I dedicate this book to my children Nick and Lianna
for their support and unconditional love.

CONTENTS

CONTACT

compassionatemedium.com

jake@compassionatemedium.com

facebook.com/compassionatemedium

914-227-5398.

ACKNOWLEDGMENTS

I would like to thank Jenn Shepherd for all of her tireless efforts in making this book happen. I would like to thank Noreen McGuire for her hard work and her special talents in editing the one or two grammatical mistakes I may have made. A special thank you to my friend Kevin Ford for giving me the push to become the Compassionate Medium. A special thank you to Jeremiah Aitken for being the light in the darkness of my unfoldment.

I would like to thank all of the teachers, tutors and mentors that have helped my development of my mediumship. A special thank you to my main teacher Janet Nohavec for creating a learning center that is unequaled in the United States. I would like to thank the many teachers from the Arthur Findlay College in Stansted England: Colin Bates, Mallory Standell, Simon James, Brian Robertson, Lionel Owen, Stella and Steven Upton, Simone Key, Paul Jacobs, Jose Gottschalk, and here in the States Rita Berkowitz and John Holland.

A special thank you to Sharon Siubis and Carole Boyce for believing in my abilities and teaching me some of the different modalities that I have learned.

A special thank you for The Lily Dale Assembly board members and the entire Lily Dale community for making me feel like "family".

A special thank you to my Spirit beloveds who work so selflessly on the otherside to bring through the everlasting bonds of love for those searching here for proof of that connection. Without my Spirit helpers I would not be able to provide the kind of readings that I have been blessed to be a part of. I also thank most humbly all of you who have sat across from me and allowed me to serve Spirit for you. It is an honor and I am most grateful for the opportunities to have been a part of "your stories", I am just the story teller, and I appreciate your trust and share your stories with the highest respect and love for you all.

.

1 BY YOUR LIGHT YOU SHALL BE KNOWN

I sat in a classroom listening to one of my favorite teachers lecturing on our own personal spirituality and he said "By your light you shall be known". He then moved on to announce that we would be breaking for lunch. As I sat and finished my lunch I realized that he had given us a gem, something more nourishing than the quick meal I had just inhaled in the short time that we were given for our midday break. What was said to us has remained with me and I thought of it often over the past few years.

As someone who is a self-taught student of history I found myself chewing up book after book about many of the old time mediums especially the British mediums. I noticed the more I learned of their personal stories and the unfoldment of their mediumship that many referred to Spirit talking to them about their light. I wondered if this was the same light that the teacher had referred to in his quote. What has been shown to me in many meditations, as well as during readings, is a sense that we are all like stars in a midnight blue black sky. Some stars shine a bit brighter than others, but all are magnificent and beautiful. The brightness of our own star is directly connected to our spirituality and how we have lived our life; the more you live a spiritual life, the brighter your star will become. If I were to use Mother Teresa as an example, the conclusion I would come to is that she may be one of the brighter stars in the sky, as she lived a life of selflessness helping all who she came in contact. She may be a bit more evolved or further on her journey than some who have passed this way. Another metaphor is that we are gardeners. The garden that we till and nurture and weed and work hard to create here on this physical plane will reap many beautiful flowers and soul nourishments when we go home to spirit. I am not saying that this is karmic: put in a bad life and have a bad eternity. What I am saying is that we are on a continuous path of fulfillment; the more you work on your own lessons here the further down your path you will be progressing.

The idea of Light and spirituality is taught to us in our youthful beginnings usually in the religious setting of our family environment and believe system. There are two things that we generally have no say about when we are born, our ethnicity and our first religion. Our parents are who they are and therefore, we are products of that union and those particular ethnicities. Most people are simply Catholic or Protestant or Jewish or Muslim or whatever religion our parents were at the time of our birth until we come of an age where we start to question what feels right for our self. Then we may choose to explore other affiliations or simply make our parents' religion our own. It is all appropriate and totally acceptable; there is no one religion that is more right or better than any of the others. It comes down to choice and the greatest gift that man has is free will and the ability to execute it.

Another meaning for 'light' that has revealed itself to me through countless readings has to do with the amount of grief and pain we are enduring. When we are so heavy with grief that spirit may choose to come through a medium to let us, their loved ones know that they are fine and still exist in the way that they are now. Many times the loved ones left behind may have been experiencing signs or feelings of their beloveds who have left this physical life around them or around other family members. I do know from personal experience that it is more likely to happen if we can lift some of the heaviness of our own grief about this loss. Easier said than done of course, the rewards of allowing our life to progress and move forward is far greater than staying in that dense quality where life is at its most difficult point for many. The point of this thought is to hopefully make us think of grieving and the loss of loved ones in the sense of a weight or burden. We can choose to stay heavy in our pain and personal suffering or we can choose to allow that for a comfortable period of time and then we can choose to move forward in our lives bringing our loved ones with us as we do. We do not let them go; we take them with us in the way that is available to us now. In our hearts, in our memories, in our photographs and a hundred other ways that keep them eternal in our journey. I repeat we do not leave them behind when we choose to move forward and live again. They are always with us, just not in the way that some of us would like.

Human beings never like to have anything taken away from them whether it is freedom or even belongings. Look at how violated people feel when their home gets robbed. Picture a toddler who has their toy taken away and the reaction is one of a sense that the end of their perfect world in that moment is over and the tantrum prevails. So now, for a moment imagine, you are an adult and somehow someone you love and value to such a high degree is taken from your not so perfect world, what is your tantrum to look like? That is the grief that we feel at that time and it is one of the most important life lessons we will ever have to experience. Life is hard and almost never fair but this is the way life is.

As is the relief of the morning, beyond the shadows of darkness brought on by the night, we awaken to knowledge of the power of the light. Our souls know before our minds, that light will always follow darkness and that darkness is not to be feared but embraced for in its quiet and solitude we meet out truest self. The self that walks the Earth without fear of judgment or containment from others ideas and opinions, is who we are and who we long to know. This is where our spark of divinity lives. This is our light that can always see us through any darkness, any despair that has been brought to us. All opportunities that come before us are lessons and patterns that we must trust are important to our spirits growth.

There are certain truths that we struggle with and for many, always continue to struggle with. This does not make one smarter than the other or more in any way than another. That is our egos when they are functioning on a lesser plane. We are all on the same spiritual journey, all beings good and evil, always moving forward often not moving in the way that we could have. You may have heard the expression, you live and die by your choices and there is some truth in that. But it is not etched in stone that we cannot go back and change a decision no matter how poor a choice or how destructive to self or others it has been. That is a component of our greatest gift, free will.

Human beings have many inherent paradoxes. Mazlov, a great man of a scientific mind, shows us in his theory that we have a have a need to affiliate with other human beings. Yet many people walking this Earth choose to live a life of solitude whether partially or wholly. Are they anomalies? Are they just antisocial? I think we have to allow for the idea of degrees of choices and not try to always look from a scientific perspective when it comes to aspects of humanalities. Would it not be accurate to say that Mazlov is correct but also accurate to say, that not all humans can be measured by the same measuring stick. That also points up the fact of free will coming into our understanding of each other which hopefully might lead to more tolerance and a less judgmental approach to each other. Just as the scientific community is now becoming open to the idea that each person is not one hundred percent masculine or one hundred percent feminine. We all have some feminine and some male qualities to different degrees. We all too often jump to judgments and say that the woman who dresses like a man is a 'butch' type and most likely a lesbian. We also see a man who has more feminine qualities and assume he is gay and fits that stereotype that we have chosen for that person. The truth be told, none of us are all man or all woman. We are many varied combinations of characteristics that make up our individualities. For all of us to move forward as a human group we must learn that loving and accepting each other may be the singular most important factor in our use of free will.

When we choose to be judgmental or intolerant of each other for whatever reason we are actually slowing down the spiritual journey of the human race. There is no punishment for this or any karmic debt to be paid. It just is what it is, a missed opportunity for man as a whole to move further along during this particular physical life experience. There is no right or wrong connected to this unless our ego decides to see it that way and then again, free will has presented another choice to be taken or even to not be taken. Very few things that we will encounter along our life's path will be black or white, light or dark, all or nothing. Almost every moment of every day that we are here alive in this physical world we will be presented with choices and opportunities for our souls to be connected. What we do at those times is where we are as spirits, having a human experience here and now. There is no right way and there is no wrong way, there just are constant opportunities for our individual and collective soul's progressions.

Many relationships struggle and some even fail because one person or one group needs to be right in a situation. I understand the need to be right. I have found that it has become far too important in our belief system. If given a choice between being right and being kind, we should choose kindness. Generally when we choose to always win the argument or prevail in the dispute we come from a place that is not close to true spiritual nature but are coming from a place of insecurity. How many marriages have suffered year in year out because one spouse needed to be right more often than to be kind to the person they have loved. I think a continual breakdown of the bond of our own true nature leads to so much of the unhappiness we see in our world today and especially in the love relationships we try to maintain and very often lose. Strive for balance of body mind and spirit. If any one of these three is not in balance, life will be a bit more difficult. When all are in alignment we live a fuller life and we are generally happier. We just have to choose. To understand that free will is always an option, and truly a blessing and a gift.

Many people nearing the end of their physical life will often talk of regrets and mistakes that they made along their life's journey. For most men it will be that they wished they had worked less and spent more time with their families. For many women who lived during the twentieth century it is that they didn't do more to establish their own place in this world. They wish they were more like the modern women we see today. After doing thousands of readings with loved ones coming through from the otherside; almost all of their regrets have to do with relationships with loved ones. The words that were said or never said, the shortage of, "I love yous" and "I'm sorrys" that were never shared are the things that are most often regretted. If you get one thing from these writings please let it be that you can say these things now don't wait until it is too late. You do not have to take your shortcomings and regrets with you to the spirit side of life. Shine your light here and now, and it will shine brighter when you leave this physical life.

How very often I hear from a spirit in a reading how much

they love their loved ones still here on the physical side of life. How many times my sitters will feel deep emotions and many times cry when they are told for one more time that they are loved by the person they miss so much. This is the truth of mediumship, this is it in its most simple form. It is the continuity of love not just the continuity of life after death, but love after death that is so very accessible for us. When a widow hears from her departed spouse that he is aware of the new grandchild and then talks about that little girl and that another is on the way, the wall between the two worlds melt away. This must be the reason a medium labors so long and so hard on their development to be a participant in yet another small miracle that is born and driven by an emotion, love.

If we understand that life is always changing then it makes sense that we must alter our ways of thinking and adjust from what was to what is, and even what could be in the future. If we deny that change is always happening we are working against the natural law. It would seem to make more sense to understand that we have loved ones near us while they are living in the physical, so why does it become a stretch for some to know that they are still with us after their passing to the spirit side of life. We are in denial of the constant inevitable change that nature has decreed. When we evolve as humans to the place where we just know that our loved ones are still alive, albeit differently, but alive none the less, then the separation from physical life to death will no longer have the strangle hold on our emotions that it has today. We live in a state contrary to natural law and this may be why we suffer loss the way that we do and it may not be necessary as our evolvement continues with our collective soul's progression.

Is your mediumship remarkable? I f you choose to sit and be passive in your mediumship it's likely that your abilities will be very limited and rarely remarkable. If you choose to believe that communing with Spirit is a one way street than you will also struggle in your abilities to provide a thorough sitting for your recipient. True natural mediumship is a multi-leveled process in which the preparation before the reading is possibly more important than the actual reading. A medium understands that they must put time into their development. You cannot go any faster in your development than what is your own natural unfoldment of mediumistic abilities. The reason many people today struggle with so called mediums or light workers is that they haven't done the work. They enjoy the attention and playing the role but they are not walking the walk but merely talking the talk. Think about it this way, who would you choose to go to, someone who has spent endless amounts of time and efforts developing their abilities or someone who hangs a shingle after taking a weekend course usually given by some medium that no longer has the abilities they once had. I would for myself always want to know where have they studied and who are their teachers.

Can you be born a medium? Absolutely! All true mediums are born to be mediums. Most rarely travel the path of a medium through most of their life. Our society makes it difficult if not impossible for a naturally born medium to live their entire life living that service. As children we soon learn that being "different' has a stiff price to pay for it, so we choose to become like the rest. Schools would struggle to allow young mediums to explore their gifts or abilities. Yes, some people may tell you that they are mediums since birth but most likely and in most cases their abilities don't usually present themselves again until they have reached a level of maturity; or for some, the depths of despair has brought their gifts to light. Sometimes when life is so hard and things have gone in such a way that one is literally at his lowest point that the mediumistic gift starts to make itself known. The spirit world will lift the veil slightly to the other side to give a glimmer of hope and show one that there is so much more than what is known at present and that glimmer will be the truest light to follow; the light that shows the way out of despair and provides the opportunity to choose to go on and possibly even to choose a life of service to spirit and fellow man. That is my story, which is how I found my mediumship or should I say, it made itself known again in my life. I am forever grateful for the reasons that got me to that point, I now understand how there is so much more to learn from life's difficult times than there is during the easy days. I do appreciate both and have not had any of the moments of despair since that reawakening, and I feel blessed.

I think we have all heard the expression "you must be present in your own life". I know I have heard it far too many times from people who were truly not present in their own lives but merely spectators to their time here in the physical world. We are in Earth School and that we have this time to learn "life lessons". From my limited but observing eyes I have noticed that far too many people are playing hooky from school. I am the last one to call anybody on this as I had plenty of days of playing hooky from high school when I was younger. The truth of the matter is that there is no truant officer or principal's office to be sent to, but there is a cost for our lack of "attendance" during our time on Earth. The price we pay is a lack of progression on our spiritual path. We all have great potential. When we play hooky we are negligent in helping all of humankind to move ahead in its progression. There is a correlation to us as individuals and us as part of a much larger whole. This is how we come to the place of saying that "we are all one, there is no separation". This may be one of the life lessons that we are all meant to participate in for the good of all. If you are playing hooky and not present in your own life as well as not present in the lives of all mankind then it is not a surprise that people struggle here in this life process. This is part of the imbalance that man feels and may add to the confusion and pettiness that exists between individuals as well as on a larger scale between countries and peoples.

Man as a whole and on an individual level is inherently good and loving. I have seen examples of this loving kindness thousands of times in my life as I am sure you have as well. My quest on this page, in this chapter, in the writing of this book is not to try and change the world by pointing out the transgressions of men. There are many others who have spent an awful lot of time doing that already. What my hope for is to strike a chord in the vibrational balance of an individual, then to collectively add to the harmonious nature of all humans. Try not to get caught up in the words that I am choosing here to express my thought but to find your own words or your own voice to make this a dialogue rather than a preachy monologue. I know that by using words like vibrational balance or harmonious nature may be a turn off to some as they sound very New Age or like a "hippy" would speak, but allow yourself to let go of that judgmental aspect and actually reflect on the feeling in the thought put forth. An easier way to understand this idea may be to think of a set of wind chimes; when one chime strikes against the clapper there is a most beautiful note; but when all of the chimes are tapping into each other and the gentle breeze creates the most gorgeous of symphonies. All that I am asking is that you listen to your own music, your own voice. You are the composer along with billions of other composers here at this exact time in history to make a beautiful orchestration, a magnificent vibration to lift the energies and spirituality of all alive at this present moment. This may be the single most common version of free will and our abilities to choose, to show up and engage in the present instead of playing hooky in our own life.

As a medium, I know that we are all students for life especially when it comes to the unfoldment of our mediumistic gifts or abilities. There is also a truth to be told about the amount of time and discipline you bring to your mediumship that directly affects your level of development. We complicate simple matters much of the time. There is nothing perfect or complete in this world until each and every one of us has touched it in some way. If we are not there, present in that moment to touch it how can we then expect things to be better or progressing. Simply put, there may be some deeper truth to the expression "you get out what you put in".

I understand how intellectuals can take a simple idea and write volumes on just a single thought, and that may be helpful for a deeper understanding. I also know that even in that process we have the opportunity for free will. The twentieth century philosopher Eric Hoffer once said "The complete works written by William Shakespeare would fill a shelf in any library, yet the books written about the works of Shakespeare could fill two libraries". If you are a dominant left brain type of personality you would probably enjoy and see great value in the works of many intellectuals who have explored and expressed their take on what Shakespeare was possibly conveying. If you are a dominant right brain type of personality you would probably gravitate towards the actual words written by his own hand and marvel at the talents of Shakespeare. But truth be told, most of us have a combination of both types of these personalities and that enables us to understand and enjoy both aspects. This is a classic example of, there is no right and there is no wrong, one way is not better than the other, all are valued and matter. The potential life lesson in this example is that it always comes down to love and acceptance. The ability as a loving gentle soul to tolerate that which we cannot relate to on a core level but accept it and understand its value and importance for others.

2 "EVERYTHING IN THE UNIVERSE IS WITHIN YOU. ASK ALL FROM YOURSELF" - RUMI

I wish I had a nickel for every time I told a client that they came here to this life with the answers to every question that will come up during their lifetime already inside of them. The key to finding these answers lies in the ability to be able to quiet our minds enough so that we may hear the answers. This is just one of the reasons meditation is so crucial for our personal spiritual growth. Today's world is a very busy place with possibly too many stimulations and distractions and it makes it much harder to be able to find that quiet time that is essential for our well-being and spiritual progression.

The word meditation seems to scare a lot of people off because of an old notion that meditation means sitting in an uncomfortable yoga position for extended periods chanting a single word or mantra. That type of meditation can be wonderful and transforming to those who are able to develop the discipline, but those are not the people I am talking to here. If you are like me; we probably will never find ourselves sitting on the floor cross legged. The type of meditation I am trying to convey here is one where you can basically do just about anywhere and for any amount of time. I even find myself drifting while on line at the supermarket.

Most of us understand the value of prayer and many of us pray on a fairly regular basis and that is wonderful. If you were like me you were raised in your early life in the religion that your parents chose. As a child we are usually taught to pray, to ask things from God, for ourselves and for others. What the old religions forget to teach us is, how we hear back from God and understand the answers to our prayers. This is where the type of meditating I am speaking about can be most helpful, in sitting in the quiet we create the atmosphere for our own true self to share things with us that are for our own higher good and the higher good of all people.

It can be as simple as this, find a comfortable place to sit, not to lie down, if you lie down you'll most likely fall asleep and as nice as a good nap can be there is a purpose to your mini retreat and you should stay awake. Once comfortable just close your eyes and allow yourself to settle into a gentle place. I choose not to have any background music playing but if you find that it helps you in this process, absolutely do it. This is your time, your special event that you are in charge. Don't concern yourself with trying to make your mind go blank or keep any thoughts from popping into your head. It is okay if things sneak in, just don't let them take over. Yes you have to do laundry and then go shopping for food for dinner. Just acknowledge and then let those thoughts go, let them pass without you following them. You will not be able to shut your mind off completely so don't even try. You would have to be a Monk meditating for a lifetime to get to that type of meditation and it is much deeper than you are going to need for your purpose of this process. If you do struggle with thoughts trying to take over your mind then do a simple technique where you just pay attention to your breathing. Hear your breathing going in and hear it going out. The reason that paying attention to your breathing connects you to your inner place is that the actual act of breathing is instinctual. We never think about breathing, we just do it, or we die. It is an unconscious act that we are now making conscious. So now when you are focusing on your breathing you are allowing a part of your brain that is connected instinctually to allow for the relaxation of your general state of being and your brain waves will alter ever so slightly in a very gentle natural way that is beneficial to your own well-being. That is the state of relaxation that is beneficial; two, three or even four times a week, whatever number of times you can do this is most helpful in rediscovering that which your higher self already knows and so graciously wants to share with you.

As you continue to meditate on a regular basis you find that it becomes invaluable in your life, learn how to relax and give yourself this wonderful gift. I prefer to call this time sitting in the quiet as opposed to meditating but you have the ability to call it whatever you would like. I have heard it said on many occasions that it takes three weeks to break or to develop a habit. What I would ask of you is that you try this exercise for at least three weeks and if after that time you choose to continue sitting in the quiet on a regular basis, congratulations! You would have created your own discipline and something very special and unique just for yourself. If you find that you need to hear a voice walk you through the steps or even to hear a guided visualization that is also fine, whatever works for you on an individual basis is perfectly fine. Try to remember, in your spirituality there are no set rules other than the ones you choose. This is something that belongs to you and you alone, not your spouse or your children or parents. This is wholly yours and you should treat it with the caring respect you would show to the most valued parts in your life.

As a medium I know that I am a student for life. There is always room for more growth both as a medium and as a person. I have been so blessed to have had and still have many different teachers to help me to grow and understand my mediumistic abilities. The gratitude I feel towards each one is heartfelt and continues to this day. There have been times that I have heard other students remark that this teacher is better than that teacher, or that they didn't learn anything in that class. I would have to say to them, wrong, wrong, wrong! That is less about the teacher than it is more about the students own perspective. I have learned something from each and every one that I have entrusted with my mediumship development. Think of yourself as a craftsman. Does the carpenter start out being an amazing cabinet maker? Or does it take a master carpenter to show him how to do things in a better or more efficient manner. You do not have to reinvent the wheel; you just have to be flexible enough in your thinking to understand how your particular wheel works. Every single teacher that crosses your path in whatever field you endeavor has shown up for a reason, there is purpose to each union of minds and usually if they are the right teachers, they are there to help you grow. I'll continue on with the idea of a carpenter since most of us understand the concept of a master craftsman. He brings with him to each job a tool box that has the right tools for the jobs he will perform. That is what you are doing as a medium. You are gathering all of the necessary tools for your individual toolbox to help you do your job well. Each teacher may add at least one or possibly more than one tool to help you in your future works. Allow the process! I am going to say it again,... allow the process. Accept what is being taught to you if it makes sense to you and it comes from a place of intelligence.

One teacher that I had early on in my development was getting on in years and people were starting to lose respect for her abilities. I saw something different in her style of teaching and it resonated with me. I chose not to judge her against what she had once been but to see her as a wealth of wisdom and information. While many of my fellow students were busy complaining about her and her doddering ways, I made a point to sit with her anytime I had the chance. When I look back over my notes that I took during her classes I do see that there is a bit of rambling in her talks, but there was also some real gems in there as well. When I would sit and have a conversation over tea between classes she shared so much of her lifetime cache of knowledge. It was in those moments that I realized that she was there to teach me some things I could not find on my own. To this day I so value the lessons I learned from her, some so basic and simplistic to others that seem to come from somewhere deeper than I could understand. She was a brilliant woman and I was so lucky to have had the chance to learn from her. She had an understanding of the importance of the relationship to spirit aspect of mediumship similar to the way a master cabinet worker is to a fine piece of wood. She knew how to make mediumship a more interactive process and less of a passive state of let me see what comes from Spirit. I asked her once how do I know if what I am getting is correct? She explained to me that she would only give a piece of information if she deemed it questionable if spirit were to give it to her three times. That was her way of pushing spirit to give her better quality evidential information. I have used this technique many times in readings over the years and it has never failed me. Had I listened to the other students I would have missed that opportunity to learn something from one of the great mediums and to add a very helpful tool to my toolbox.

You can learn from everyone. All people have the potential to be teachers in life's journey, but for that to work one must show up for school. The very fact that you have picked up this book shows that you are interested in the potential to learn something. For that I applaud you. Most people live a better and happier life if they continue to educate themselves, whether they choose formal education or the route that was a better fit for me, to self-educate. When you are choosing to keep learning you are deciding to keep your brain active and your mind stays open a little more. As a medium I also have learned that once spirit has given you something they will never take it away. If you are mostly clairsentient in your mediumship you will always have the ability for there to be more feeling in your mediumship. Now, the even more interesting part of this scenario is that spirit will work with you individually to bring out your other abilities as well. You may find that one day you are not feeling the energy the way you did previously and it makes you nervous. Well, if you can trust that spirit knows what they are doing I promise you that they are going to expand your other senses. You may start to become more clairvoyant, see pictures in your mind's eye or possibly even with your eyes open. That is how they train us and if you are in a constant state of trying to control your gifts you will be limited in how you can work with spirit. Allow through trust, that spirit will add another tool to your mediumistic toolbox.

The relationship we have with spirit when we work as mediums is an interactive mutually nurturing one. The bottom line is that spirit needs people on Earth to be available for communications. They simply need more employees to work on their behalf. It is an honor to be chosen to do this type of service and a responsibility on our part to put in the hours of work on our spirituality and our mediumship. Please don't ever take this too lightly, this is one of the times that the old maxim is true, what you put in is what you get out. If you are lazy or decide to take the easy way in your mediumship it will become evident to all that you are just not able to deliver the quality that is needed to show the continuity of life after death but even more importantly, to show the continuity of love after death. . Of course there are plenty of psychics and mediums who forget the work ethics needed for great mediumship. They make the rest of the mediums pay the price in the eyes of the public when they deliver mediocre mediumship. Always try to show up to serve with the right reasons in your heart, come from a place of love and do what you can to help the suffering of another human being. It is one of the highest most humbling honors to participate in these small miracles. In truth, aren't all miracles really small, except to the person in need of that miracle? For me, this is the highest calling when we choose to serve those who need that miracle. Be worthy of that.

3 "DOESN'T EVERYONE DESERVE AT LEAST ONE CALL BACK HOME?" BRIAN ROBERTSON, OSNU

You may already be aware that there are many different types of mediumship that has been practiced throughout history. I am only going to concern you with mental mediumship and in a more specific version which is evidential mental mediumship. Mental mediumship is devoid of any physical manifestations or any trance components; it basically means a mind to mind connection between the physical world (here) and the spirit world (the otherside). In this connection there is communication from spirit to the humans here and the purpose is to show the continuity of life. That is the most widely held explanation of this type of mediumship. If you are seeing a medium for a reading in this present day the medium is probably using this method. The true reason for anyone to engage in mediumship today whether as a sitter or a medium, is to bring through evidence of the continuity of love not just that our loved ones still exist in a different way; but in fact they still are connected to us through the bond of love that existed between us and them. I believe this to be the truest and highest form of mediumship available in today's world. This is the type that I have worked hard to achieve and if you are a medium reading this, I hope this is what you will be striving for within your own personal mediumistic abilities. If you are someone who is looking for a great reading from a medium be prepared before you go to your session.

The sitter is the recipient of the reading. An easy way to

understand the process in a very simple analogy is that of a phone call. The spirit loved one makes the call, the medium is the phone booth and the sitter answers the phone. The medium has a special job in this method of communication, to make the connection to the spirit and deliver the messages from loved one on the otherside to another loved one still here in the physical world. I often tell my clients that there is nothing special about me, but there is something special that I can do. Mediumship is never to be about the medium. It is always about creating a connection from one world to another. If it seems like it is more about the medium than what I have described, then the medium is operating from a place of ego and not serving spirit in the purest form, and I am sorry that they are the ambassadors of the spirit world and you have been short changed in your opportunity in your reading. Good mediums understand that this gift of mediumship is sacred and meant as a way of serving both the spirit world and their fellow human beings.

When choosing a medium to do a reading for you it is your responsibility to find the one that is the right fit for you. Ask other people who have had readings; were they happy with their reading? Would they recommend that particular medium? All mediums except for celebrity mediums live and die by their reputations. Mediums that become what I refer to as celebrity mediums are essential to the work of spirit as they are the ones that draw attention to the need for mediumship readings. Are they actually better than other working mediums? I say no, they are usually not better in the quality of their readings, but they are much more marketable in a commercial sense. They serve a purpose in mass marketing the idea of spirit communication but there is a downside to their version of mediumship. Most of the time that you see them on television they are doing a public demonstration of mediumship which is rarely as evidential as a private reading. Some even practice a form of cold reading. A cold reading is when they give out vague or general information and then use that to connect to an audience member that would love to hear from someone in spirit. Now, they are working with someone I would refer to as a true believer, this person is not using enough of their God given common sense at that moment to have a healthy dose of skepticism working for them. They are vulnerable to the stage presence and persona of the celebrity. This can be very engaging for the audience and even somewhat helpful and evidential for the recipient but it is not mediumship at its purest level. It is not for the highest good of all involved but mostly for the financial benefit of a few. Like many things in this modern world celebrity mediums are a double edge sword. If you have actually thought about it most celebrity mediums seem to have a shelf life and then fade away. My personal belief is that spirit will make use of people like this to get a wider base of interest but generally their abilities tend to lesson with over exposure similar to what happened in the past with physical mediumship.

In the nineteenth century which is often referred to as the beginnings of modern mediumship, physical mediumship was more prevalent. As the phenomena of physical mediumship became more popular the demand for it grew with the public. Again the double edged sword, the mediums could not produce at the rate of what the public demanded. Basic laws of business apply here. The law of supply and demand came into play, the more the public demanded seeing with their own two eyes the more the mediums had to supply. Mediumship is not meant to be used in that way, that often. So in the long run, the demand for this type of mediumship from the public ended up killing off physical mediumship. The mediums resorted to trickery and even some acts of fraud by some of the more unscrupulous mediums.

My understanding of mediumship is more in line with that of

the British mediums of the twentieth century. More emphasis is placed on the direct connection of your own spiritual growth while you are unfolding your mediumistic abilities. Modern mediumship may have started here in the United States but for the last eighty years or so it has found its roots planted in England. As the physical mediumship declined in value it too declined in the eyes of the public and spirit replaced it with mental mediumship and that has become the staple of mediumship worldwide. That is not to say that there still isn't physical mediumship still happening today, because it does still happen just not nearly as often or of the same quality of its heyday. It takes a tremendous amount of energy to produce physical phenomena and people of this modern era do not have the time or discipline to sit in a spirit circle for the good of a single medium for years, week in week out and many times without seeing results for years. We need to remember that a hundred years ago there was no television or radio, and people had less distractions overall. So to choose to sit in a circle with your neighbors or a relative was like an evening out. Here in the United States, at the beginning of the 1900s there were over ten million members in Spiritualist churches. With a population at that time of just over one hundred and twenty million that meant that one out of every twelve Americans was a Spiritualist. One of the main components to the Spiritualist religion is the practice of mediumship. Sitting in a séance or spirit development circle was part of pop culture at the time, and on the whole it was free because there were no expenses other than snacks after the circles. For many, just a cheap night out.

4 "PAINT THE DECEASED LOVED ONES BACK TO LIFE" – JANET NOHAVEC

No two mediums are alike. All mediums work with some commonalities but there will always be differences from medium to medium. If we are to believe that a mediums abilities in providing connections and messages to and from the otherside, are as different as snowflakes gently coming down from the heavens then we need to understand why all are different, yet all are valued and serve a purpose. The level and quality of one's mediumship is directly connected to one's spiritual place and it changes as one unfolds gifts and as one works on personal spirit growth. No one starts at the same place and no one ends at the same place so it is logical to conclude that no two mediums will ever be the same. So I pose this question, why do so many young mediums try to be like other mediums? I think the answer may be found in a lack of confidence in the gifts he or she has and perhaps a lack of trust that spirit will hold up their end of the bargain. Trust of spirit is a main component of mediumship. The sitter must trust that the medium is gifted and connected to the otherside. The medium must trust that the spirit communicators will show up and provide the feelings, pictures, sounds, smells, tastes and whatever else spirit has to paint the story of the spirit communicator back to life for the sitter.

My main teacher for many years has and still is Janet Nohavec. Janet is a former Catholic nun who many people believe to be the standard bearer for the quality of evidential mediumship in the United States. She has told her students during many lessons that it is the job of the medium to use words to paint the person back to life. Those of us lucky enough to have found Janet as our teacher have come to learn that discipline and hard work are the building blocks on which the foundation of mediumship is built. Mediumship can be a hobby for many, but those that put in the time and effort it becomes more than a hobby, it is a lifestyle; a way to live life, a roadmap for spiritual growth and an opportunity to serve others. That is what the old timers used to refer to as a calling. I am honored to have been chosen.

I find myself smiling sometimes when I get into conversations with mediums starting out who think that they have stumbled onto something unique. In their limited vision and immature approach to mediumship they have yet to come to the truth that they have been chosen by spirit to do this work. If they need to have their ego stroked then they may even believe that they are special because spirit has chosen them to work with spirit. But they would be dead wrong, excuse the pun! I promise you, and I have said this countless times to sitters and groups, there is nothing special about me, the medium. Yet there is something special that I can do. It is never about the medium, it is about the love connection between this world and the spirit world. All human beings have their own issues. Welcome to being human! To be a great medium means you have put enough work into your own issues and personality flaws so that you are able to move yourself out of the process so that spirit can use what you have to provide the link between the two worlds. If you have things you need to work on then get to it. Get it done so that you can become the best employee you can be for spirit. Yes, I said employee. I am an employee for spirit. The clients may pay me but I work for spirit.

If you are someone who needs to please people, please don't

become a medium unless you can remove that people pleasing part of your personality. It will only get in the way of real mediumship. Sitters sometimes show up wanting something, or to hear from one particular spirit in a reading and this can actually hurt what a reading is able to accomplish. I always explain to my sitters that spirit will always give what is needed, not necessarily what is wanted. Much of the time allowing the process to unfold without any preconceptions will allow for both needs and wants to be fulfilled. Many people go through life having issues with control. A medium with control issues will have a hard time working with spirit. A sitter trying to control the reading will most likely end up sabotaging the reading. The truth of the matter is that the medium controls the way the sitting will go, but the spirit world has always been in control of the bigger picture of the reading. Spirit will often arrange for the sitter and the medium to find each other. I find that spirit gets involved long before the appointment for the reading is ever scheduled. I will take it a bit further by stating that sometimes spirit will even choose the medium for that particular sitter. There have been times when I do six or seven readings in a row, one after another, and by the time I am finished I know exactly who I was supposed to be there for that day. Sitters come for readings for various reasons; there is a sincere need, a curiosity. Some of the time they were even dragged there by their spouse! I know that the best readings are when there is a true need, but let me say this so you get the point I am trying to make here, ALL readings are valuable. There is a purpose to all mediumship if it comes from a place of intelligence, and there is intelligence in the spirit world.

There are ways to get you the best reading one can receive at that moment. I always ask my sitters to set an intention for their reading before I start and if time is available and they have a prearranged appointment to set their intention by asking their spirit loved ones to come to me. My thought is, loved ones in spirit do not know me. They are your loved ones so please ask them to come to me. It is a polite and respectful way to approach the spirit world. Just as I set my intention before each reading by asking that the reading be healing and meaningful and come from a place of love, and that the reading be for the highest good for all. I remind my sitters to be open to who come through. It may be a neighbor from down the street that you knew when you were a little child and you barely remember. You may want desperately to hear from someone that is closer to you. I remind sitters that every spirit that shows up deserves an opportunity to be acknowledged and be remembered. For all we know that may be the only time that spirit gets a chance to reach back through the veil between the two worlds and who are we to deny them their chance? If you are unhappy about who comes through then you are probably not showing up with an open heart and an open mind which are essential for you to get a quality reading. The loved ones that you are really hoping to come through will invariably show up in your reading anyway. For all we know that old neighbor of yours was the person who was acting as a gatekeeper and will bring your people through so again, try not to be controlling in your reading. Spirit knows what it is doing and you need to trust the process, after all spirit has been doing this type of communication forever and you are just a beginner so be respectful and allow them to bring you what you need. It is for your higher good. I can also tell you with great confidence that the more love you are feeling when you come to your reading will have a positive effect on your reading. Love is the fuel that drives the mediumship train. Please show up with a full tank.

As a working medium I understand the value of showing up prepared for your reading. I have spent years honing the craft of interpreting different energies. I will never show up and not have my energy to the level that is necessary to bring you the best reading for you. I am able to raise my vibration, spirit operates on a higher vibration so they lower theirs and with your energy I am able to get to where your loved ones are. My own energy will only take me so far, I need your energy to raise it to the place where you will get the quality of the reading we are both working to achieve. My teacher Janet Nohavec often refers to this as the perfect cocktail. My energy, your energy and spirit's energy blending together is the formula for a reading. Many mediums from days gone by refer to a mediumistic reading as 'the grand experiment' as it is never the same twice. Sometimes someone will show up for a reading and they are still in work mode or they just left their significant other after having an argument and their energy is not right at that moment for a reading. On occasion I have been able to sit with sitters for a moment and shift the energy to the place it needs to be to achieve a proper blending. There have also been times when the sitter's energy is just not conducive to connecting with spirit and I will postpone the reading for another time. I would rather not give a lesser quality reading. An experience with the spirit world needs to be healing and loving, not filled with disappointment. I am the ambassador for the spirit world here on Earth at the moment of a reading and I have prepared to work for them for the good of all. The last thing I want is to facilitate a mediocre reading. Sitters need to understand, that this is the mentality of what a good medium needs to bring to the table. Look for this when choosing a medium to visit with your loved ones in spirit. Most mediums live and die in a business sense by their reputations and word of mouth advertising. Try to find your medium from someone who has already had a reading from them or look at the testimonials on their website to see if they feel like a good fit for you. If you are in an area where you don't have access to quality mediums, then a place like Lily Dale may be a good resource for you to find your medium. Remember even in a place like Lily Dale there will always be varying degrees of mediumistic abilities, but it almost always come down to this, is this medium the right reader at this moment for this sitter? Just as there is chemistry in love relationships, there must be chemistry between the sitter and the medium. You will understand that better after your reading or after you have had numerous readings with different mediums. Trust your gut instinct when choosing your medium!

5 TAKING ONE'S SELF TO THE OTHERSIDE

In a reading that I was giving to a middle aged mother who had lost her adult daughter by suicide, I saw the most incredible visual in which the young woman was standing in what to me seemed like a school science lab. She was standing at a lab table and in front of her were the most beautiful yet miniature animals. I knew that they were full grown, alive in every way but none were any larger than two inches in height or about the size of a small field mouse. I saw a rabbit, a puppy, a kitten, a deer, and a lamb. Can I explain this logically? Hardly. I was just amazed at how gentle this young woman was in handling each of them and how careful she was that she paid attention to each one in such a loving and compassionate manner. It was a very emotional visual for me. Just being a witness to this interaction between these very small and fragile animals and this young woman who had chosen to leave the physical world made me feel that I was participating as a spectator to a form of care that was being shown. I don't know how to explain it in any other way. About six months later I was reading a book about a very famous British medium from the nineteen thirties named Gladys Leonard and in this book she describes basically the same scene also having to do with a younger person who took their own life. Ms. Leonard's explanation of why the animals were so tiny and so vulnerable had much to do with the way the young suicide victim had seen themselves. Here they were being given the opportunity to care for something so much more vulnerable than themselves. I believe that spirit was using these animals to teach the young woman about caring for something outside of herself. In using these very small and gentle animals it gave her the chance to see that there was no threat from them and that they needed her, which made her feel that she mattered to something and that she had value. This may seem like such a small lesson but I think it is a major gift that spirit used to start the rebuilding of a soul that had been through such a difficult physical existence. Spirit was treating her the same way that she was treating these little animals, with pure unconditional love and total compassion. Spirit uses her choice to pass as an opportunity for her spirit to grow. There was no judgment or sense of negativity in any way connected to her suicide, there was just love and compassion as if one part of a whole was taking care of another part of that same whole. This is a great example that we are all one and that we are all always connected. This may be how we can come to understand the value of unconditional love and the need to live our lives sharing unconditional love with all people. When in doubt, love is always the answer. If you are not sure how to respond in a situation, pour more love on it. Love is our life line and our light out of any darkness; even in suicide there is light.

I have read in many books about differing versions of what happens to a person who takes their own life. Here is my belief which I state emphatically: the person who commits suicide does not experience it the way you think they do. It has been shown to me in countless readings for families of suicide deaths that the loved one who takes their own life never experiences the pain of the event. Their spirit is removed before the act is fulfilled. I get the same visual when a person dies in an accident that is violent. They love us so much in the spirit world they take us out of our bodies so that we do not feel the pain; I repeat, our loved ones never feel the pain that you may think was associated with their passing. It is like a wisp of air leaving the physical body at the exact moment, the very last second before the trauma would be experienced. That is how much we are loved by our beloveds in the spirit world.

In a reading I once gave to a widow of a September 11th victim it was shown to me that he never felt the pain that she thought he might in the last seconds of his life. The visual I saw in my mind's eye was one of many spirits lifting up and away from the tower as it came down to the ground. He showed me that at the time of his passing he was doing what he loved to be doing. He was an emergency service police officer leaning over someone having a heart attack in the stairwell of the 22nd floor of the first tower. I did not know if what he was showing me was evidential until after her reading his widow shared that his body had been found in the rubble where the number 22 was written on a large piece of debris. For me, I understood at that moment what a hero is, someone who acts out of pure love even though they may lose their own life trying to help a fellow human being, and sadly in his case, he did lose his life. Some people are built to run towards danger and most of us are built to run the other way. I have a tremendous respect and admiration for those who have the calling to help us at our most desperate times. I believe that their spirit chose that path for them before they were ever born and it is their destiny to help all of humanity even at the potential cost of the loss of their own life. I also appreciate the level of love and commitment that it takes to be part of a family that has these people in it. You know every time they walk out the front door that they may not be walking back into your arms again. There is a reason these types of couples find each other and I can also understand why they can be some of the most difficult relationships to be involved in. Blessings to those who live that life, and thank you for being the care takers of all of us, we are all one family.

I have been touched numerous times in my own life by the sadness of someone taking their own life. It is always a profound and heart wrenching experience for all of the people that are connected to them, none more so than the loved ones closest to them: their parents, their children, their siblings and countless others. Having done scores of readings where loved ones have come through who have taken themselves over to the other side, I feel that I can speak with some degree of certainty. I have never, even once, had a spirit of a suicide victim come through without having regretted the action of their final event here in the physical. There is always an apology connected to taking responsibility for what they have done. I believe that through a sort of life review they are shown in a very loving and caretaking way the effects of their final action.

I use the term life review because it is the closest wording I can find to try and explain the process I have come to understand. I have been shown by spirit that when we pass from this world to the next we all experience this life review type of process. It is not like seeing your life pass before your eyes but more like that of a gentle but enveloping process that shows every interaction you have experienced in your physical life, both good and bad. All are learning opportunities that have been brought before us by spirit or by our own free will. All are necessary to our spirit's growth and should be looked at with open eyes and not from a place of fear or karmic payback. That is not real to the process, but rather something created by humans long ago to find power over the masses of people on Earth at different times in our history. That would make this process a fear based event but what I am speaking of here is based in love, not fear.

As we come to understand our roles in each of these interactions we are able to see how our choices at the time caused a ripple effect and that we have responsibility for all of our choices.

For example, let's say you are a child in school and you kick a boy in your class, and that boy then goes home and beats his little sister because he can. As that young girl grows up she chooses men in her life that do not treat her well and may even hurt her physically with violence. On some level you own a piece of that because you kicked that little boy and started the whole process of hurting her soul that day when you were just a small child. We are responsible for all of our actions in our life, every single one. Does that mean you will be punished for that kick that led to the later difficulties in her life? No, it doesn't work that way. Rather, there is an opportunity for each and every participant to learn something. You could have not kicked that boy, that boy could have chosen to not take it out on his sister. His sister could have chosen better people to bring into her life and rejected the victim mentality that she chose in our fictitious story. We each have free will working with us many, many times each and every single day of our life. The lesson here is to stop and try to understand that we cannot control the actions of others but we can control our reactions in situations. This is one of the grandest ways that spirit shows unconditional love to each of us. We always have choices to make. There is never a void of opportunities for our spirits to grow, even in the worst of times.

I can also attest to the loving, gentle care that is shown to the souls that have taken themselves away from the physical world. Many of the old time mediums from the last hundred years or so have seen similar versions of this care. I have even read where they interpret those souls being cared for in a hospital type of setting until they are well enough to move on their continuous journey. I have never had that sense, but I do relate to the feeling of compassion brought out in that explanation. The bottom line is that there is unconditional love given to all people when they pass, even the ones that are judged here for their actions in a less than loving way. We should never judge the actions of one who has done this.

Yes, we may go through a phase where we feel some anger towards them for their choices. That is probably not something you want to hang on to for too long. As in most grieving, our anger will pass. This will happen as we process through our own minds and hearts and come to understand just how much pain and suffering they were living with. This time in the physical life can be just too difficult for some people. They may not be equipped with enough of the coping skills to see them through their perceived inadequacies and the difficulties that will arise in their life. We should strive to show them love at all times, both here while they struggle, and after they have made their choice to leave here. We all have heard the old saying, judge not a man until you have walked a mile in his shoes. If we were as quick to offer love as we are to offer judgment this world would be a gentler place for many who struggle.

In the year that I was testing to become a registered medium at Lily Dale, I was serving spirit to a group at an outdoor service at The Forest Temple. If you are not someone who is used to standing up in front of crowds in public this can be a very nerve wracking experience. On top of it all, you have to trust that spirit is going to provide you with the messages for someone in attendance who hopes to connect to their loved ones in spirit. An actor standing on a stage, or a singer about to perform or even more so a comedian about to do their routine can relate to the fear of being vulnerable and exposed at that moment in front of a large group of strangers. But an actor has lines memorized, as does the singer who knows their songs, and comedians will rely on the jokes and stories they tell to win over their audience. A medium has none of the above. We walk out in front of this crowd of strangers hoping to hear from someone they miss so terribly, with nothing but our faith in our relationship to spirit that will bring forth the comfort and proof of the continuity of love between the two worlds. This is why a true medium spends their life in service.

With almost every appearance at the forty public outdoor services I served that summer at Lily Dale, my name was butchered by the chairpersons. It sort of became a running joke all summer and I found it to be helpful in the long run as the audience could relate to me and it almost always raised the energy of the group with the laugh that it produced. One day, as I made my way to the front, I immediately felt the presence of a younger male in spirit who wanted to connect to his mom who was sitting in the audience. So I spoke, "I have a younger man in spirit with me here who wants to speak to his mom, not his mother but his mom, you would know the difference, he is also telling me that his name is Nick and that he left behind a little boy who you love very much, he is also telling me that the name of Jean or Joan would be significant to you. He is also telling me that he is taking responsibility for his passing". In the group of a couple hundred people, one little shaking hand rose and I immediately knew that this was his mom because I felt a wave of love rush through my body. He so wanted to hug his mom. I continued, "this is your son Nick? she responded "Yes" I could see her emotions rising and I knew tears would be falling very soon. I said to her that "I feel as if I am woozy or that I may be under the influence of drugs or too much alcohol," she said she understood that. I then said to her that, "he wants you to know that he is fine, he did not experience his passing the way you believed he did. He felt no pain." She started to cry. I continued, "I'm not sure why he is showing me that he is looking at water but I don't feel he got wet." She said she understood why I felt that. I continued on to give her more information about what was current in her life and how much he loved her and was sorry for what he had done and for the pain that she felt by him taking his life. I was very careful how to word things since we were in a public forum and it was just so personal and private that it truly was not anyone else's business but hers. She composed herself enough to let me know that her name was Jeannie and her son who committed suicide was named Nick and he left her a beautiful little grandson.

There weren't too many dry eyes in that group that day and I know that the message that came through for that brokenhearted mom that day was transformative to her life. I spoke with her after the service concluded and she told me that her son had found his way back to drug addiction after being sober for a few years and that he had taken himself to a bridge over a river and leapt to his death. His body had been found on the cement foundation of the bridge, he had not made it into the water. I sat with this mom for about an hour and had a conversation about her Nick and her grandson. I asked, as I often do in private readings, "what are you doing now to take care of yourself?" This is why I believe mediumship, when done at the higher level is an interactive and learning experience for all involved including the medium. She told me that she is active in working with families that have also had loved ones take their own life. She could have spent the rest of her life being angry or victimized by her son's act of desperation, but instead she chooses to help others so that their burden of grief may be just a bit lighter so they can move forward in their lives. To me, she was an angel walking the Earth. If you need to understand compassion and grief, sit and have a conversation with someone like this mom. It will change your life and make you a better person, and that is how you can take a horrible negative episode and turn it into a life-transforming positive life lesson. I believe that Jeannie and Nick will be together again one day, and I know that he is alive in her heart and in her memories. That is her miracle created by free will and the wisdom to understand the lesson presented to her. That is what I believe a more evolved soul is like here in the physical world.

In many of the readings that I do for grieving family members, I have noticed that the more difficult their passing, the more I will receive their information through clairvoyance. I will see more visual cues to interpret as opposed to just having a sense of something as in clairsentient download of information. I believe that spirit does this so that I may choose my words more sensitively in my explanations to the recipients of their information. I tell everyone I read that the impressions or thoughts that I receive from spirit are always correct. My interpretations can be wrong, I am human and can often make a mistake in the way that I express spirit's message or impart a certain piece of information. This is one of the reasons I record every single private reading I do on a CD for the sitter. I think that many people in the moment of a mediumship reading are touching energy they are not used to and may miss some of what has been given. I know by giving them this CD for them to listen to again and again in the future they will always understand what they were given by spirit. It allows the sitter the ability to stay present in the moment of their reading to fully feel the connection to their loved ones. The other reason I find recording readings so valuable is that it holds the medium to a higher standard. You own every word that comes out of your mouth. The last thing I want is for when I die to have a bunch of spirits asking me why I said all these wrong things to their loved ones. As a credible medium I stand behind every word that comes out of my mouth with integrity.

Interestingly, I have seen some of the most enlightening visuals when I was in connection to a spirit that had taken their own life. A common theme in many of the visuals with these spirits has to do with activities that they are now participating in. I have seen them sitting in great marble lecture halls with hundreds of other spirits. I have seen them in scenes of nature that I would understand. Do I believe that nature where they are is the same as nature that we have here on this planet in this physical world? No. I believe that they show me these things so that I may understand what it is like for them in a way that my brain can wrap around. I once saw a young man who had taken his life sitting on the back of a tram similar to the ones they have at Disney World that delivers you from the long distances of the parking areas to the front gates of the theme park. When I saw this young man sitting on the back of this tram, in a mind to mind conversation I asked him, "what are you doing?" He replied "I am going somewhere; I said, "You are? Where are you going?" he answered back, "I am going to listen to music." I asked, "What's with the tram?" He said "That is for you, so that you understand that I am in motion. that I can go places." I understood what he meant. I asked him who he was going to listen to. He said, "Nickleback". And with that the visual stopped. I had heard the name of the band Nickleback but had never heard their music, and to be honest with you, I knew this young man in spirit and knew that he liked heavy metal, head banging type of music. It got the best of me, so the next morning I went online and found videos by the band Nickleback. I looked down the list of their videos and one seemed to draw me to it and it was called "Someday." I clicked on it, and was astonished at what I was watching. The video was very much about proving the continuity of life after death. It just amazes me the lengths that spirit will go to in order that their messages get to us. Of course my rational thinking mind knows that this young man in spirit probably did not ride a tram to a Nickleback concert here in the physical world. The part of my mind that is connected to the spirit world understood the value of what he was trying to convey to me in showing me that visual. That life is continuous and there are signs showing us this in so many places, if only we opened our minds to them. It was a beautiful gift that he chose to share with me from the otherside.

On another occasion I saw that same spirit at the edge of a creek bed and he was handling the smallest most beautifully colored frog. It was a most vibrant, almost fluorescent green with some shade of bright red on the back of its head. I thought it so beautiful even though I am not one who chooses to touch most small animals. I am the type that has someone else put their worm on the hook when I go fishing. I am a city boy at heart. As I saw this young man in sprit holding and communing with this frog, I felt there was a true sense of love and care from him to the frog, as if it was his job to show love to this animal and to be concerned with its well-being. As he gently placed the frog back onto a smooth wet rock about a foot off the shoreline into the creek he then turned and walked away along the edge of the creek and the visual ended. Over the next three or four days I must have seen more than a dozen small frogs with red on the back of their heads either in photos, in print advertisements or in television commercials. I believe in synchronicity and do not see these events as just a coincidence. I understand that we are given lessons over and over in our life. For me the gentleness of how he handled that frog and the feeling of love that he showed that amphibian was a reminder for me to stop and smell the roses, to be aware of that which surrounds us in beauty, and in nature. It was another gift from him in spirit.

The very first time that I saw this young man after his passing, he appeared to me through clairvoyance. I saw him with my eyes open. Earlier that day I had been writing a poem and my mind drifted to him. In my thoughts I found that i was asking him, what is it like from behind your eyes? Much to my surprise my writing took much longer than usual. When I read the poem afterwards I felt like I had written the first quarter of the poem, and the last part as well, but the middle of the poem felt like it was not mine. Even the words that I wrote were words that were not of my usual vocabulary. I understand now that it may have been inspired writing with an influence from the spirit world, or possibly this young man expressing thoughts he wanted to share. I'll never truly know until I meet up with him again someday. That poem can be found in the back of this book.

Later that day I was at home and found that I had time to take a short nap before I needed to start cooking dinner for myself and my kids. It was a very cold wintry January day about five weeks since this young man took his life. As I climbed into bed, before I had closed my eyes, I was no longer in my room, but rather was part of a scene that has changed my life forever. With my eyes wide open this is what I saw: I found myself standing on a small hill and about a hundred yards away I could see a horse fence with a beautiful meadow beyond it. In front of the fence was a long pebbled path that wound down to my right. On this path I saw this young man standing and staring into the meadow. He looked back over his left shoulder and said, "It's good, I'm good." As he spoke to me his face was no further away from me than two feet, yet I knew he was a hundred yards away a second ago. Of course I was amazed at seeing him but what was more amazing to me was the way he looked. He looked like the most beautiful version of himself. His face was clean shaven and full and his complexion was creamy and he looked better than I had ever seen him when he was alive. Just as fast as he was there in my face he was now back on the path. I looked at the horse fence and I noticed I could see the grain of the wood as if it was only a foot or so away from my eyes, then I could see the underside of the wood and now the other side of the wood. How was I doing this? I had not moved but somehow the fence had moved. I looked into the meadow and was just blown away by the colors of the grass; I noted that I could see both sides of the gently swaying grass. The vibrancy of the colors was not like anything I had ever seen before or since. The colors in that scene were just beyond description in words that I knew. It was more beautiful and breathtaking than anything I can describe to you even now, years later. As my eyes drew back to my friend I saw him take a few steps along the path and I remember telling myself to memorize what I was seeing as even while in it I knew something special was happening. He turned again and said something that made no sense to me but I remember it even now. What he said to me was very personal to his mother and I have promised her that I would never share that message with anyone and so I will respect her wishes. What I can tell you was that it was validation to her that her son was fine and he was alive but living in a different place. It was a life-transforming event for all of us involved, his mother, me, and him. In that moment, I knew that life was continuous, that we don't truly die in the way that I had believed. That was my first experience with communication from the otherside.

I liken that first experience of communication with a spirit to a dam being broken open and the water starting to flow. From that day forward something more came from spirit each and every day. I thought for sure that I had had a psychotic break because I was seeing visions and hearing someone else's thoughts in my head. I knew a professional in the psychiatric field and I had a conversation with her. I needed to know if what was happening was the onset of mental illness or was truly happening. She explained to me that when they do an intake of someone who is being evaluated for a psychotic episode there was a series of questions. She asked me those questions and I answered them and her conclusion was that I was perfectly normal with no signs of psychosis. I looked at her and asked her, "Who was Dolly and why is Dolly in the sewer?" I told her I saw a large man trying to lift off a sewer grate and fish out a small doll. This professional woman with all these many years of training melted right in front of me. Tears welled up in her eyes. It turned out that when she was three years old she and her dad had been walking in the town where they lived and her doll fell out of her hand and fell down a sewer. She said, as tears now fell from her eyes that this was her earliest childhood memory and she could not understand how I could know this. Well, that made two of us!

One amazing discovery that has presented itself to me many times in readings of people who have taken themselves to spirit is that they often explain the experience of their death as a happy accident. I know that sounds incredibly strange, so let me explain it in the way that it has been portrayed to me. Many times when people have been in the actual act of committing suicide, they relay that there is a point where you can still stop your death from happening. All too often, however, persons taking their own lives are under the influence of either too much alcohol or drugs and this can dull their reaction time. What has been shown to me repeatedly is that at a certain point in the act of their suicide people will try to stop the action of whatever method they have chosen to use to end their life. When their inability to stop the event from happening occurs, usually because of the influence of drugs or alcohol, there is a line that gets crossed and the momentum of the act carries them to that final conclusion. The commonality in this type of circumstance is that they did try to stop their suicide but their judgment was impaired and they died. They don't refer to it to me as an act of suicide but as a happy accident.

Once they recognize that there is no chance of turning back they just accept their decision and face it with a sense of uneasy happiness. They seem to think of it as an accident since they did try to stop it. What I believe happens with them as they go to the otherside is that they are shown the consequences of their actions and the pain and hurt that it has left with the people who care about them. That is when I understand it becomes real to them and not the illusion they have bought into of a happy accident. That is when the healing begins for them, for it wasn't their physical life they needed to end, but the life they were living and struggling with needed to end. You do not have to kill yourself to end your life. It is a perception issue. Yes the life you were living needs to end but you do not have to die for that to happen. You need to change something drastically. Anything short of taking your own life is acceptable. Walk out the door and just keep going. Start over, reinvent yourself. Don't worry about the hows and wheres and whys; just walk away from that life that was killing you literally. I promise you that you never have to take your own life. There is always a choice and the decision to let your old life die is okay, but your body should stay alive and start again in a rebirth of your time here in the physical world. Suicide is a permanent option and one that does not have to be chosen no matter how bad things get. Understand that in the moment before the act of suicide that one is not thinking with a rational mind; that one is as unstable at that exact moment as a human being can be. If you are feeling this way, walk away from your own thoughts and just keep walking until a shift in your thinking or perception happens, and it will always happen, always. You do not have to die to end the life that makes you miserable. Do not do it, just walk away.

Of the far too many readings that I have done involving a spirit that was responsible for their own passing, I have never had one come back and say that they were glad they did it and that it was the right decision. Never once! They almost always come back to say that they made a mistake and that they were sorry for the pain that their death caused their beloveds left behind. There is always a sense of regret and always apologies given. One of the cruelest parts to a suicide that I believe is partly what elicit the regretful feelings from the departed, is that they have taught the generation behind them that taking your own life is an option. The rate of suicidal deaths is higher in families where there has already been a suicide. The rate of copycat suicides is markedly increased in families where there has been a previous suicide, especially among younger teenagers and siblings of the departed. This may be one legacy in families where suicides have happened that needs to be addressed but all too often families tend to feel shame about the way their loved one died and people just don't seem to speak about it, and that is wrong and sometimes deadly wrong. If your family has experienced a loss by suicide, please make sure that it is discussed and that attention is paid to those who may be vulnerable.

People are inherently kind and loving by nature and we come around for those that we care about when a tragic passing happens and that is the right thing to do. Sometimes as the dust settles we go back to our own lives and soon forget the impact of the pain from a suicidal death that was left to the loved ones or we are aware, but it is just too hard or uncomfortable to keep touching that hurt. It is in those moments that we as fellow human beings must step up and do the right thing even though it may make us uncomfortable or uneasy. For this is the time that spirit has given to us to rebuild the bonds of love that have been damaged by the act of an individual who was not in their right mind and definitely not thinking clearly. Draw those loved ones that are the most damaged closer to you. This is the time they need more love and more compassion and it is within our abilities to care for them at their lowest points in their own lives. They are truly the victims in this scenario, not the person who took their own life. The ones left behind are the ones who now suffer. I have found in my limited experience that this is the time to simply pour more love on these souls; they need what we can give them: unconditional love. I also promise you that every ounce of love that you choose to share with someone at this point will come back to you tenfold. It will cost you nothing, but will mean the world to them. Be humane not just human.

A thought that I would like to impress on you is the importance of love and tolerance, or actually the lack of enough love and tolerance in our society and the problems created by these deficiencies. I recently did a reading with a middle-aged woman and what came through during her reading was that her younger brother, years before, had taken his own life in a violent fashion. He gave his sister evidence as to what happened and how he was doing at this point more than thirty years after his suicide. He was an excellent communicator. He very openly showed me something that was a well hidden family secret. He was a service man, proudly on a tour of duty in a foreign country and fell in love with a fellow service man. Their homosexual relationship became known and he was humiliated and abused for the relationship that he was involved in. This is what led him to take his own life. He was just eighteen years old, alone in a foreign land without the love and support he needed in that moment, and he made the choice to hang himself. This was during the days of the widespread panic about the AIDS virus. The sense of shame about being who he was and the feeling that he would never be accepted for who his true self was, added to the depressive state that he fell deeply into. He came through in his sister's reading with remorse about his actions and also a sense of regret that he wished he had been born at a different time, in today's time. As a people we are still progressing and evolving to a place where people of the same sex can love each other without the scorn or maltreatment of others. Is this world that evolved yet? Not really, but it is much more accepting and tolerant than it was thirty years ago. What this beautiful young spirit shared with me that day had rarely been spoken about in this woman's family. They still carried the shame of how he died and for the reason he chose to leave here. This reading was transformative in her life as she was finally able to hear her brother openly talk about this event and that part of his physical life through me, a stranger, a non-family member. The wall of shame was broken that day by this brave soul. Weeks after her reading, I received a phone call from that woman. She told me how healing and helpful that reading had been for her and that her family was now openly talking about her brother's death and, more importantly, about his life. He finally found the love and support he needed. Even in his death this spirit was able to help his family evolve and progress by taking the first step to effecting the conversation that was so long overdue. Ironically, his passing was the same year that Ronald Reagan said "Tear down that wall Mr. Gorbachev." This beautiful soul from the other side tore down his family's wall. I was proud to touch his energy. Simply said, love is love, who are we to judge?

6 "OUR BIRTH IS BUT A SLEEP AND A FORGETTING" – WILLIAM WORDSWORTH

For as long as man has been able to think one of the questions he asks is where did I come from? Philosophers and theologians have spent lifetimes trying to find THE answer. The simple truth is, there is no one answer! For as different as we are as individuals so are the different truths that are real to us. Black and white thinkers would have you believe that there must only be one truth. I believe that each of us has a truth that we contain within our own understanding of life. What is true for me may not be true for you. For example, if I say that I know that stealing is wrong then that is a true thought for me. If someone steals food for their children because they are going to die from starvation, they may likely believe it is not stealing because their children would die otherwise. I am not talking about what is right or wrong. I am using this example to show how the truth is relative to the individual. If I were to take this thought process a step further, I would then say that stealing is always wrong, however, that mother who is trying to keep her children alive is dealing on an instinctual level and not on an intellectual level, and might say that her children dying from starvation is more wrong. Then it becomes an intellectual exercise in futility because now we are no longer exploring the idea of truth but rather definitions of truth and who sets the standard for what is true.

Understand that it is right to reach for answers to all of life's questions, but also understand that it is alright that not all of the questions will have answers. It is one of the great paradoxes of the human experience. If you come to sit at the table of humanity, come prepared to accept all who sit with you, and all of their differences. Accept and marvel at difference, for that is the true nature of human beings. We are all one; all parts that make up a greater whole. If you struggle as we humans do, with the differences of others, you are in truth struggling with that which you are a part of. That may be a universal truth as opposed to a perceptual truth that we spoke of in the paragraph above. Come to understand more about your own truths as we move forward.

I agree with what Wordsworth said in his quote, "Our birth is but a sleep and a forgetting," I have come to this resolution as a medium, because I know that life is eternal going forward and so, I believe that life has been eternal going backwards. We have always been and we shall always be. What may be difficult for some to wrap their minds around is that which science can now show proof of: eternal existence. From Einstein's Theory of Relativity and the continued works of countless physicists regarding quantum physics and even more specifically dark matter, we know that energy can never be destroyed. Human beings are energetic based life forms. Yes, the physical envelope that houses our spirit and soul will have a certain lifespan, different for each of us, but the truth is, our bodies will die, but we do not die. The essence of what makes up a person is not just their body. There are many components that are also part of the human being.

Our spirit, that which was with us before this physical life and that which will live on after this physical life has ended here on earth. This spirit, the goodness of our soul, will come with us as we move forward on our progression. Many of the characteristics that made up our personality in our life may still be part of our soul progression. Many times there are things about us that are unique and quirky that may have been parts of us before this lifetime. An example of continuing traits may be the explanation of the term "old soul." Have you ever met a young person and they just seem to be wise beyond their years? Or just have a certain assuredness about the way they carry themselves? That may be because they have an "old soul". There are many experts out there for you to read or hear from about past life regressions or forms of reincarnation. All that I am trying to do here is to ask you to think about it, to dwell in the land of "what ifs?" if you don't believe it already. You may find the answers to some of life's truths.

It has been shown to me over and over again in readings that there is proof of life being continuous after our passing from this life to the next. We can stop here and choose to be satisfied that we have taken a perceptual truth and shown it to be a universal truth however, we can also ask, "So what? So what that life is continuous? What is the purpose of proving the continuity of life if we do not come to an understanding of the intelligence behind it?" What I think is that it is only the first truth to be realized and that there are probably many others to yet be uncovered or proven. The bold statement I am making is that for there to be life after physical death, there must be intelligence in the spirit world. That is where I believe the real value in connection to the spirit world lies. Not just in the messages, as wonderful and transformative as they can be, but in the actual mind to mind communication that is the thread that weaves all of us into the tapestry of eternity. This is yet another reason to value quiet reflective time, meditation to some. Just to sit and ponder the questions that lead us to our own truths and the truths that were there before us and will be there after we no longer walk this planet.

You were born with the answers to every question that will

arise in your lifetime already inside of you. You will only hear those answers when you are able to quiet your thinking mind just enough for your soul to connect to your mind. This is the part of all human beings that connects us to the mystical side of our spirit. This is the part that is sometimes referred to as our spark of the divine that resides within our soul. If you believe in God, or the Source, or Great Spirit, or the One, whatever term that resonates with you about the higher power that we are all a part of and that is a part of us, this is your spark of divinity. Come to a place of understanding of how truly important your role is in the bigger picture. You matter and always have. You are a valued member in the eternal family. If you recognize that you are an important part of this family then it will also be clearer to you that you are never alone or of little value. Those are issues that are manmade and are of this physical life.

As we settle into the twenty first century, there seems to be shift in the thinking of some people. Many new agers call this the awakening which comfortably relates back to the Wordsworth quote earlier. I tend to think of it as a paradigm shift more in line with the sense of a pendulum that has swung too far in one direction but now seeks to balance itself by swinging back in the other direction. The key word here is balance. I know that individuals when not in balance of body mind and spirit tend to have a more difficult time here in this physical life. So it comes as no shock that the state of the world at this point being in some type of disarray, is out of balance; and the world in its current state is one full of strife and difficulties. If I were to stop there our situation might seem hopeless and futile and life as we know it might just not seem worth the effort. I, however see it as another opportunity for the growth of all people all over this world. In the many readings I have given over the years I have yet to see struggle in the afterlife. As far I as I can tell, it just does not exist there, it is an earth-bound problem.

The world and its people at this time in history are out of balance. So now, what can we as individuals do to be a positive part of the change that is needed? Before we can become agents of change on a global basis we must become agents for change in our own lives. We must become responsible for our own lives and then to accept responsibility for each other as part of the eternal family. I know that some of you may be rolling your eyes about now thinking, "Here we go, this is the do-gooder who is going to change the world with his idealistic ideas." Yet, that couldn't be farther from the truth. I don't believe the world is ready yet for the type of change, and change on the scale, that would be necessary. I think it will be more of an evolutionary process over time.

I heard of a family in a town not far from where I was living, and their elderly mother had wandered off and had been missing for a number of days. I decided to see if I had any abilities that might help in locating this lady. I had not been contacted by the authorities or by the family, so I knew on some level that I was in that gray area of not being within the boundaries of ethics relating to mediumship.

I sat and just opened up with my thoughts focused on this elderly woman. What I felt was her energy as that of a child's energy. I saw her walking in the town after midnight with a sense of purpose. She was looking for a place to go swimming, she was feeling hot and wanted to cool off by going swimming and in the town where she lived there was a pond. A moment later I felt her resting, lying down in some soft grass and falling asleep very gently. At that point I believed that she had passed from this physical life and I was no longer connected to her. I have never shared that story with anyone and have always wrestled with the ethics of whether I should have made an effort to follow up on my "feelings."

The conclusion to this story is that the lady's body was found lying in a bed of grass near a large river in the town where she lived. She had been dead for a couple of days by then and was discovered by someone walking their dog in a public park, only a five minute walk from where her family lived. I had been right in some of my information, but I had her going to the other body of water in her town. My information would not have been helpful to the authorities or to her family except in sharing with them what I believed her last moments were like. She had passed away very peacefully and in a childlike state mentally. I share this story with you so that you understand that as gifted as one may believe themselves to be, you must always be cognizant that there are essential rules and ethics that guide psychic work and mediumship. Recall the saying regarding physicians; it can also apply for mediums, "First do no harm!" Had my ego gotten involved and had I chosen to make this scenario about me instead of what it really was about, a family in the midst of a crisis, it would have been wrong. I was not fully correct in what I had gotten, and it would have misled their investigation and it would have been wrong for me to approach them. That being said, if they had approached me and asked for help, I would have readily given them what I got and it would not have changed the outcome, but I would have stayed within the boundaries that I have set for myself, and I would not have come from the wrong place in sharing with them.

Boundaries in mediumship are essential to the core of what a credible medium does. This is one of the reasons so many teachers and mystics talk about removing one's own ego from the process of spirit communication. Far too many people who try to work with the spirit side of life have not done enough work on themselves to truly be of the highest value to spirit. The best mediums are the ones who have spent years working on their own psychological issues and neuroses. You must be balanced in your body, mind, and spirit to be of the highest use for those in the spirit world. It doesn't mean that you have to be a perfect human species to do mediumship. It does mean that you need to check your own issues before you choose to represent the spirits in communications with others. All people are a work in progress and all mediums are students for life. Those are facts and I see them as positives and not as negatives. Speaking for myself, I have had a love for learning throughout my whole life. The subjects have changed over the years but the desire to keep learning and growing intellectually has never diminished. Think of it this way, the more you have in your brain the more spirit has to work with to bring through information and messages. I happen to be a very visual person who has been fortunate enough to have been born with a good degree of creativity. That is what spirit uses to imprint visuals and thoughts to me. All of my life I have been a fan of films. It is my hobby and I probably see between seventy five and one hundred films a year in the movie theaters. I am lucky that where I live there are a few art house type movie theaters and many that that run inexpensive showings at certain times of the week. Those are the times that I can afford my hobby.

The reason I mention this is that very often in private readings and sometimes in public demonstrations of mediumship I will be shown a certain scene or a character that leads to a piece of evidential information for my recipient. For example, during a reading at an outdoor service at Lily Dale I was giving a message to a gentleman in the audience and I saw the television character Archie Bunker from the series, "All in the Family". I went on to describe his father's personality based on the television characters personality and it was spot on for that man's dad. Right down to an apology for not being more kind to his son that he treated like a "meathead." Later that night at another event that I was serving spirit at, this same gentleman and his wife approached me to say how transforming that apology was from his not so easy going dad. Not only did they make my day by being kind enough to share their emotions about what had transpired, but I felt such a wave of love come through me for this very large man in his fifties who was sobbing like a little boy because he finally had been given the closure he needed to childhood pain. Had I not been trained well as a medium I could possibly have dismissed the visual I was seeing as my own imagination and this joyful family reunion would not have taken place. Both this man and his wife bear hugged me in gratitude but the truth of the matter is, they were hugging his dad for stepping up and becoming the man he was not able to be when he was still in the living. I was grateful to the spirit world because it helped me to see more of the humanity of people both here and on the spirit side of life.

As an aside, I would like to add that I have found that many times when dads and also moms who were difficult in family situations here on the physical side of life come through, it seems to me that it is very important for them to show their loved ones here in the living how much they have grown on a spiritual level. I believe that is why there are so many apologies and regrets about things said or left unsaid. We here still in the living should allow for the opportunities for our loved ones to open up and share these new sides to their spiritual personas. We all have an understanding of what a family unit is like but the truth of the matter is many of us are not realistic of what our families are really like. Hollywood and especially the television industry have sold us a version that is far from most people's realities. I don't know about you but my parents were nothing like June and Ward Cleaver on Leave it to Beaver, or Howard and Marion Cunningham on Happy Days. My parents both worked very hard and had four boys to raise and plenty of bills to pay. They didn't have time for the sensitive interactions that were portrayed by these fictitious television families. They were people doing the best they could based on their own histories and the failings of their own upbringings. One thing I know as an absolute, children do not come with a how to manual attached to their umbilical cord. Again I draw you back to what I had said before, that it always comes down to love and acceptance. Finding the right balance is what allows us to grow as individual spirits and as spirits belonging to a much larger whole.

Another absolute that I know to be true is that when in spirit communications our beloveds on the otherside have shown me more times than I can count that, the only thing that truly matters is the love bond in our relationships. That is what survives from this world to the next. There are no material things there, there are no religions there; there are no political ideologies there, what there is that matters and is valued is the loving and compassionate feelings that connect all of us whether we are in the living or in spirit. It seems to me that the more we chase the things in the material world the further we are from our true selves which distances us from our beloveds who have transitioned to the otherside. The term family values have been talked about so often and so much by so many people with agendas, they may have actually created a tuning out of what family values truly are. Love and respect for each other, whether we are related by blood or members of the universal family. Love has and always will be the glue that binds all people together. We came from love, we go home to love. We just have to learn to love each other while we are here.

7 "ETERNITY STARTED LONG BEFORE YOU FOUND IT" -JAKE SAMOYEDNY

For some reason people tend to think that eternity is something that starts when you die. That same logic would lead us to believe that the sun never existed until it rose in the morning. Neither would be true statements. For me, the word eternity is of the same value as the word infinite, meaning no ending. I also believe that it could be interpreted as also having no beginning. Some truths cannot be explained by the words that we have in our languages. If you say that you believe in a God, Higher Power, The Source, The One, whatever name you are comfortable with to explain something greater than yourself that exists for all time, then I ask that you open your mind to the idea that there are things that we are not equipped at this time in our evolution to understand. We may collectively as the human race one day evolve to the point that we can understand all that is available to us. I know that through the communications with spirit of credible mediums, we are moving in that direction and that it is directly connected to our spiritual growth as a people.

You don't have to be psychic to see the future, you just have to have an open mind and the future will show itself to you. I cannot predict the future and honestly I don't believe anyone truly can. We have free will, and the ability to make decisions and choices second by second constantly alters the future so it is really not possible for someone to predict it. I do believe that there are people with an incredible gift of intuition that are able to identify certain events or happenings that may occur such as earthquakes or other natural occurrences. Many times the laws of probabilities can explain the predictions that some celebrity psychics make. Be skeptical of seers and fortune tellers because often what they are able to predict is that your wallet will become lighter after they finish with you. Always rely on your common sense when dealing with someone charging you a fee to tell you about your life. It is usually more about your desires for quick answers to questions that will unfold naturally anyway with time. If you learn to be a more patient person you may find that you don't really have a need for a fortune teller.

I recently had a conversation with a young man who had lost his dad to a violent suicide. In an attempt to try and understand the why and how of what had taken place with his dad, he went to one of those storefront gypsy psychics that we see in strip malls all over the east coast of the United States, looking for answers. He was a young man of means and I'm sure they were able to size him up fairly quickly when he arrived at their place in a very expensive automobile. I knew his dad as a distant relative of mine and my mother had called and asked me to go over and try to comfort the family. After I had an in depth conversation with the widow, the young man asked me if he could talk to me in private in his room. When alone, he confided in me that he was going to a certain psychic and that in the four visits he had made to their establishment, he had handed over two thousand dollars. He was expected to return the next day with another fifteen hundred dollars and a rock that he produced from his pocket. When I asked him what the stone was for, he told me that there was a curse on his family and that is why his dad killed himself and this particular blessed stone could gather up the curse and only this psychic could remove the curse from that rock. I asked him, how they knew his dad committed suicide. He said he told them his story and then he asked them why his dad did this terrible thing. On top of all of that, they also told him that he was likely to do a similar thing if he didn't have this curse removed. Of course they could remove this horrible deadly curse, as long as he paid them the money to lift it. People like this are not psychics; they are nothing but frauds that prey on vulnerable hurting people. I had a long conversation with him and made him promise me that he would never go back to those people again. I had him put my personal phone number into his cell phone and told him he could call me anytime he needed to, not because I wanted to be a hero, but because it was the right thing to do. The bigger lesson for him in all of this was to know that there were people in this world he could trust. We then went outside and he threw the rock as far as he could into the woods. That was a turning point for him and he returned to college and got on with his healing and his life.

I followed up with a phone call to a friend in law enforcement and sadly that woman moved on before they were able to catch up with her. Please understand that criminals like this have nothing to do with the spirit world or trying to help their fellow person, they are simply thieves who have figured out a scam that works over and over on people who are at a very low point in their lives.

There are always lessons to be learned even in the worst of situations. This is why places like Lily Dale and Spiritualist churches are so valuable to meeting the needs of people in trouble. You will never hear of anything underhanded or illegal connected to a place like Lily Dale. They spend a tremendous effort to test not only the abilities of their registered mediums, but also their ethics and morals. That is why Lily Dale has survived and prospered in meeting the needs of its guests for over one hundred and thirty five years and will be around for many, many more.

A common mistake that I have noticed with mediums during their development, is not actually understanding the process of what they are participating. If you were to stand back and see what it is that is occurring, you may come to realize that it is nothing short of a small miracle. Someone in the living physical world is in communication with someone who has died and no longer lives in the physical world. How do we mediums do it? To be honest with you, I am not one hundred percent sure how it happens. There is a genuine air of mystery attached to the process. As a medium, I know the journey that I have taken to make myself available for this use by those in spirit. Anyone who tells you that they have a clear cut understanding of this process is probably not being honest with themselves. I believe that we have ideas of how it works and why, but one overall definitive answer, I don't think anyone can give that to you.

No two mediums are alike. We all start at a different point. We all develop our gifts to different degrees. What is integral to the process of mediumship is a list of certain commonalities. There is a direct indisputable link between your own personal spiritual development and how gifted you are as a medium. If you are someone who has undertaken your spiritual journey and is learning about the many differing modalities connected to spirituality and living a more spiritual life, you are more likely to become a more developed medium that will be able to bring through better quality communication. I also know that if you do not make time to meditate or as I have been trained: "to sit in the power," you will struggle with your development. Being able to "sit in the power" is the equivalent to charging your battery so that your engine can run longer and stronger. It can be considered the fuel of mediumship. Most developed mediums will sit daily or, at the very least, as many times per week as their schedules will allow. To be a quality medium you must become quiet enough in your mind to be able to hear the messages and information that spirit is trying to share. This thought leads me to a quick lesson about the different ways mediums get their information.

Remember, no two mediums are alike, so no two mediums will receive information in exactly the same way. There are the basic "clairs", as I call them. There is clairvoyance meaning clear seeing, either subjective that only that person can see something or objective which means others can see it as well. There is clairaudient meaning one hears it, and there is clairsentient meaning one feels it. There are many other subcategories of each of these modalities; however, I'll stick with just these for now. Most mediums are dominantly clairsentient in the way that they receive information and messages. They have a feeling that leads them to a choice of descriptive words to use so that you understand what information is being given to you from the spirit world. When a medium is working clairsentient you will hear them say phrases like, "I am sensing" or "I feel like", or "what is being impressed on me." Always pay attention to the phrasing of a medium when they are working. If you do you will likely understand which ability is being used at which time. If a medium says, "I am being shown" or "I am seeing", they are most likely receiving clairvoyantly at that moment. If they say, "I hear them calling out this name from the other side" or "they are telling me," then they are most likely working clairaudient in that moment. Most mediums will bounce around with all of these techniques during your reading but predominantly they will be receiving the information for you clairsentient. If a medium becomes lazy during their development they will rely mainly on only one of the "clairs" and not develop the other gifts that may be available to them. Mediums are human beings and we hate to look foolish and get things wrong, but we all do look foolish sometimes. I promise you that we all make mistakes during your readings. I trust that the information that I am receiving from spirit is always correct, and I will give it to my recipient without editing it. Where I can look foolish or be incorrect is in my interpretation. The imprint I get from spirit is correct, but I as a human then have to interpret the sometimes tiniest piece of information.

Many times there are multiple ways you can interpret a piece of evidential information that is pertinent to the sitter. In a very recent reading, what I saw was a New York Yankee baseball cap, but I knew it was an old version and not a modern version of their caps. So I said to the client as I was communicating with his dad in spirit, "I believe your dad was a NY Yankee fan." My sitter said "No, not really." I then thought maybe he was giving me a shared memory of something he and his son had done together like going to a Yankee baseball game. The son said, "Well, he only took me once. He didn't really like sporting events and big crowds." Had I not had the experience that I do after doing so many readings over time, I may have been stymied. Instead, I asked, "Is there any other way you could interpret this old time Yankee baseball cap?" He said, "My father's uncle once had a tryout with the Yankees back in the days when Babe Ruth played for them." As soon as he said that it just felt right and I knew that that was the piece of information his father was using to prove that it was him communicating since there could be no way I would ever know a family fact like that. This is one of the reasons why I always try to teach my sitters how to be a part of their reading. As a medium of integrity I want the reading to be the absolute best reading I can give at that moment. That is my goal each and every reading. What I have learned through trial and error is that the quality of a reading has more to do with the sitter's energy than mine. I am a professional so my energy is where it needs to be for a reading. I know that spirit is ready because they start before I even sit with a client to give me bits and pieces of information. Basically, spirit is nudging me to get to work for them, in a very loving caring way. I have always maintained that those in the spirit world want to connect to you just as much as, if not more than, you want to connect to them! So the only part of this "grand experiment" that can throw off the reading is the sitter. Again, all mediums have their own ways of working. Written here is what I have found to work best for me at this point, and I'm sure I will be honing it and tweaking it for the rest of my life: I always instruct my sitter, that's you, to arrive for the reading with an open mind and an open heart. I also ask that you ask your loved ones to come to me. Remember, I am a stranger to them and this is the way you set your intention with the spirit world for communication using me as your medium. Think of it this way, your loved ones in spirit world want to call you here back in the physical world so they have found a special phone booth, which is me, that can place that call for them which you then answer. It truly is as simple as that.

What I then share with sitters is that, at this point, I am blending with spirit first and then with them, so I need to build the energy as strongly as possible. The only way I can do this is with my sitter's help. One of my teachers always refers to a reading as "mixing a cocktail"; it is never the same twice. It is different each time because of the three different components involved and any variable has influence on the reading. I always ask my sitters to help me build the energy by being as positive as possible, especially in the first few minutes of their reading. I will tell them if I am wrong about something I bring forward, please don't say, "NO! NO! NO!" That just kills the energy and I then have to spend time building it back up. So what I ask them to do , even if they are one hundred percent sure that I am incorrect, is to just say something neutral like, "I'm going to think about that" or "I'll remember you said that". That way the energy keeps building and it always hits that zone where the reading just flies and we tend to get those "Wow" moments. This has not failed me so far, and the times that I believe the readings weren't as wonderful as they could have been were usually because the sitter was not open to the communication or was there with an agenda.

Interestingly enough many of the times that the sitters have said, "No" it turned out later that it was actually correct, but they were not aware of that information at that time. This is called "validation after the reading." It is the best version of evidential mediumship. In many books by mediums, including this one, we tend to share some of our best work. Now, I am going to share my worst reading to date.

Many times I get called to go to someone's home and they host an evening of readings with family members or friends. I generally do six or seven readings in a night and they are supposed to be thirty minutes each; many times they run a bit longer especially if there is a real need and the possibility of a real healing for someone. The way it usually works is that the participants gather and make an evening of it in another part of the house while I am in a room where there is privacy and I read each person individually. I record every reading I do onto a CD so that the sitter may listen to it in the future; knowing this can keep them from being distracted by taking notes during their reading. I also find that once a medium records all of their readings, the quality of their mediumship rises as they become more aware of how important everything that comes out of their mouth is and that they are responsible for every word. The recording of the CD is also helpful because of what I refer to as "sitter's amnesia." People tend to forget things in a reading that they wouldn't normally forget. I can't tell you how many emails or calls I receive days and weeks after readings where the sitter reminds me of something I said to them that they said "No" to during their reading, but once they had thought about it more they realized what I said was correct. I have even had mothers who forgot their baby's birthday, and a wife who forgot her deceased husband's name. There is something about touching the energy of the spirit world that can just throw some people off.

This particular evening, I was in this beautiful upscale home in the suburbs outside of New York City; I was there to do six readings. All was going well until my third sitter came in. His body language was that of someone who definitely did not want to be there: arms folded and a face that looked annoyed before I even made a connection to spirit. I have worked with skeptics before so I wasn't worried. I went into his reading and brought through an uncle who had passed when he was a boy. I told him his uncle's name and that he was a competitive body builder and the sitter replied, "Yes" to all of that information. Then, all of a sudden, I felt my energy being pulled away from me. I stopped for a moment and looked at him and asked him, "Are you trying to read me?" He said, "You have three kids and you're having problems with one of them right now." I asked him, "What are you doing?" He said, "Anyone can do this. It's just feelings and deductions." Then he added, "And your marriage is on the rocks." That's when I stopped him because he obviously didn't understand what he was doing and had no concept of boundaries. I told him, "It's my job to read for you, let me do my job." I went back into the reading and told him his mother was here and that her name was Bernice and that she had struggled with cancer that had spread very rapidly through her body. I looked to him for affirmation of what I was saying so that I could draw his mother closer and give him a meaningful reading. He looked at me and said "I was right, huh?" That's when I stopped and told him that the reading was over and that there would be no charge since this was not working. I told him I would be happy to try another time if he would accept and respect the way this works. His ego was so huge that he still wanted to know if he was right in what he said about me having three kids, one in trouble, and about my marriage also being in trouble. I told him not to quit his day job as I was a single parent, divorced for nearly twenty years, and had raised my two children who were both doing just fine at that time. So no, he didn't get one thing correct but what he did do was, he did me a great favor because I used that opportunity to learn how to control my readings better after that. I was a bit angry initially when this happened but quickly composed myself as I had three other readings to do that night and I could not let the arrogance of this gentleman ruin the chances for these people to connect to their loved ones. He was just one of those guys that wanted to go into work Monday morning and tell his coworkers how he was a better psychic than the psychic at this house. I felt bad for him because he actually missed an opportunity to hear from his mom in the spirit world. Maybe this would be the only chance she would get to connect back to this world. I don't know, but I did feel sad for him. I also heard from the host of the gathering that his wife was very embarrassed by his behavior in front of their friends. As I do live a spiritual life, I would not deny this person a reading in the future if he ever requested one again. I like to believe that all people are capable of growth and maturity. If I were to get on my high horse and hold a grudge about his behavior that night then I would be coming from a place of ego and that never works out well for anyone especially a medium.

I hope I have helped you understand better how mediumship can work. To get the best reading possible, as a sitter, you need to choose the right medium for you and you need to be open to the small miracle of communication between two worlds and to leave your ego out of the process. Keep in mind that your loved ones in spirit want to connect to you in the ways that they can now, just as much as, and sometimes even more than, you want to connect to them. I truly believe what one of my teachers Brian

Robertson says, "Doesn't everyone deserve at least one call back home?"

8 "NOW IS THE WINTER OF OUR DISCONTENT" -WILLIAM SHAKESPEAR, RICHARD III

There is another "clair" that doesn't seem to get much attention from most mediums and writers on mediumship; I call it "clairdelusional." All mediums have worked under this heading during their training and, hopefully, less and less as their development unfolds. This is when you are simply making things up or the information is coming from your imagination and not from the spirit world. There is a very big step in a medium's development where you stop just believing what you are getting is from spirit and you instead know when it is from spirit. When it is a belief there is always room for doubt; when it is a knowing, there is no doubt at all. This is where true mediumship sets it's rudder for the journey of the soul to soul connection and mind to mind communication. This is the standard of mediumship that a medium should aspire. An example of a "clairdelusional" reading is something like this: "I have a woman with me who is saying that she is from your mother's side of the house. I see her in an apron and I smell cookies baking in the oven. She loves you very much and just misses you so much and wants to hug you to pieces." Even though this is an uplifting message, where is the proof of evidence so that you know who this spirit is? There are no names and there is no idea of the relationship of the spirit to the recipient. This generic description could fit so many different people that have passed over. Almost all of us know someone who loved us and baked cookies. How did the woman die? Is she with anyone in the spirit world or is she alone? Was she ill for a long time? or did she go quickly in her passing? Those are all things that spirit will provide in a real mediumship reading with a true connection from the spirit world to our physical world. Do not accept anything less than intelligent proof of the continuity of life in the spirit world.

At an outdoor service at The Inspiration Stump in Lily Dale, America's oldest Spiritualist community, I was serving spirit and I heard a visiting medium say to a very young audience member, "I have a man with me named George who says that you don't know him and that he was from the seventeenth century and he is here with a message of support and hope for you and he is offering advice about your education." This medium was severely "clairdelusional". There was absolutely no intelligence to him bringing a message from someone from four hundred years ago who this person could never have known. Why would he think she should take his uplifting message and advice? This type of medium is a danger to unsuspecting people and should never be allowed to give messages in front of the public especially while working under the auspices of a great place like Lily Dale. Had I been the chairperson that particular day at The Stump I would have stopped him and apologized to the audience and then I would have made sure that the young girl got a real spirit message so that her impression of mediumship would not be one based on a dishonest person's imagination. Trust your own "gut" feelings; if it doesn't feel real, it probably is not real.

We must always come from a place of common sense and with a good dose of healthy skepticism when attending public demonstrations of mediumship and message giving. As for that medium, I'm sure our paths will cross again one day and I will take the time to share with him my thoughts on that type of message-given in the hope that he will try to become a better ambassador for the spirit world. For many people at that service that day; it may have been their first experience with spirit communication and I would never want them to think that what they saw was the standard for mediumship. It was not. It had absolutely nothing to do with mediumship at all. It was just someone taking advantage of an opportunity to stand up in front of a couple of hundred people, and put attention on himself. There was no service to spirit in what he did. All real mediums are ambassadors for the spirit world and must always try to conduct themselves with reverence for the responsibilities that come with the role. Mediums are the employees for the spirit world. That man should have been fired!

Mediumship and most things associated with spirit connections will, at times, attract people who are not mentally or emotionally stable. As a medium, this means sometimes you have to size someone up fairly quickly and do your best to help them without becoming too overly involved with them. I have tremendous empathy for people suffering with mental and emotional illnesses. But I also know that I am not qualified to deal with them in any way other than to be empathetic to them. There are professionals out there who have trained to help these individuals. I keep a list of some that I can use for referrals if I perceive the need.

Many times during a reading with a private client I will hear from spirit that there is a concern that needs to be talked about and I will shift my energy that way. Sometimes it can be magical and inspire a thoughtful conversation, and other times it is just good old fashioned common sense advice that the person needs at that moment. I am not trained to do therapy or counseling and I am very upfront about that. Often I become aware that this person who has sought help from those who loved them the most in their life just need someone to remind them that they matter and that what they say and feel is important. Most truly gifted mediums are naturally good listeners.

In far too many readings spirit will come through and let me know that this person is in trouble and needs someone to help them get back on track in their life. I see this conversation as an opportunity for a paradigm shift. I will spend extra time talking with the sitter and usually do a follow up phone call just to see if they are trying to take their life back or if they are choosing to continue down the path of self-destructive behavior. I cannot live their life for them, just as I cannot get in the way of their personal journey. I would be doing them a huge disservice if I got in the way of natural order. I could possibly be denying them the opportunity for a life lesson to be learned. No one gets out of this life without a story. Every story is important and must have the chance to happen and unfold as it is meant to. Where I observe many people struggle is when they start to believe that their own story is everyone's reality. No matter who is giving you life advice, whether it is a trained professional, a caring friend or even a medium, always use your own intuition to see if it feels right to you. No one outside of yourself knows you as well as you do. Try to step back and look at what is being offered from a place of common sense. You were born with enough of it so why not use it?

I have made a point during my development to only focus on one aspect of service to spirit. This is a good fit for me and the way my gifts are unfolding. There are so many different modalities and I have studied most of them at least on a surface level and others more in depth. For myself, and please remember, no two mediums are the same, so I can only speak about this from my perspective, I choose to only do mental mediumship; mind to mind communication from our physical world to the spirit world. I am trained and qualified to do other modalities as well but have made a conscious choice to become a specialist in just this one area and I believe that spirit has understood my desire to work this way and my level of mediumship abilities continues to grow and expand.

For some reason it has always bothered me when someone gives me their business card and it lists everything under the sun that they claim they can do because they took some courses in them, whether it is Reiki, or Qi Gong, or dowsing, or any of the other scrying modalities such as Tarot or Angel cards. How could someone become totally committed and proficient enough for me to trust their ability if they are all over the place with their energies? I understand the desire to learn these other ways to serve spirit; I just think that a more focused approach serves the public better. My guess is that some practitioners believe that by working in more of these modalities they will cast a wider net and serve more clients. When you choose to work with so many types of modalities I believe that it may work against your potential. Do I believe you should not do these things? No. I think it is fine to do as many as you would like, but only after you have concentrated enough on one that you are proficient to serve the public's need. I will use the example of a shotgun, when the trigger is pulled its buckshot goes in many different directions and may hit the target because of its blanketing effect, but it is an ineffective way to hunt. Not that I am a hunter, I'm not. I prefer to use a laser approach in my choice of working and would choose a high powered rifle that hits a pinpoint target without the collateral mess that buckshot leaves. That is how I approach my mediumship with spirit. I am the laser shot looking for the best evidence to show continuity of life after death, and not giving out random fluffy messages.

Is there value in all types of mediumship? Even the fluffy message type? Yes. I believe all mediumship has value because no one has the right to decide what is valuable to another when it comes from spirit as long as there is a real connection to spirit and meaningful healing communication coming from the spirit side of life. I just happen to prefer the better quality standard in my own style mediumship and I do not accept lesser standards when someone is giving me a message supposedly from one of my beloveds in spirit. I always advise clients to be skeptical but not critical or shut off to the process. To always look for the intelligence in what is coming from spirit. Messages from spirit are usually about how much they still love us, they miss us. They are still around us in the ways that they can be now. If a spirit message is brought through from a medium that says that the spirit is stuck in between worlds or that they are going to haunt your house now and make you life a living hell similar to the hell they are in now. I would advise you to get away from that alleged medium as fast as possible because they are not mentally stable.

All credible trained mediums will tell you that there is no such thing as spirits being caught between worlds. They are not ever in a "hell" on the otherside. If they belonged to you, why would they want to haunt you and make your life miserable? This is all craziness brought about by unscrupulous people posing as mediums to get attention and probably your money. Hollywood has taken the beauty and natural wonder of mind to mind spirit communication and bundled it into the world of the occult and they could not be any further from each other in reality than that combination. Steven Spielberg is a wonderful film maker and story teller but he is not qualified in any way to show you the afterlife. He sells fiction and his job is to put people in the seats at movie theaters and scare them, and he is great at that job. I am a big fan of many of his projects but I would not choose his version of what ifs to sell tickets. There is absolutely no connection to the real workings of the spirit world and what Hollywood is selling us. I know that many people make a living "helping people over to the otherside" as they are stuck. Absolute nonsense, but it does play into people's nature to want to be scared of the unknown. Otherwise there wouldn't be the rides at theme parks that millions run to every year to scream and cause their adrenaline to race throughout their bodies.

There is a component to human beings that loves to be scared of what is unseen that is why we believe that there are ghosts and haunted houses. What is the intelligence behind these haunting and ghostly apparitions? Why does this ghost need to appear at that particular time and to that particular person or people? I do believe that spirit can manifest in some ways that are difficult to explain. I have seen with my eyes open spirit beings moving around in a very methodical non-threatening way. My thoughts on these few "sightings" is that energy can never be destroyed so in a way there is a "stain" of that spirit that can be seen by some but usually not many people. An experiment you can try with your friends is to have one person stand against a white back ground like a wall with their arms stretched out like a cross. The other people can be on the other side of the room observing. At a certain point the person standing against the wall will go to the floor as quickly as possible and the people observing will stay focused on the spot on the wall where the person stood. There will still be an imprint of the energy of that person for a second or two. That is what a ghost is like, an imprint of residual energy. Can it hurt you? No, it is not physical and it wouldn't want to hurt you anyways. The film Poltergeist from the mid nineteen eighties created a whole new set of false fears for that generation and generations to come. Sayings like "go to the light Carolann'" have become part of the conversation to many Americans. The truth of the matter is it was just a well-made scary movie, nothing more than that. As a matter of fact the word poltergeist is a German word that means "noisy spirit". Couldn't the "noisy spirit" just be a communication from the otherside to the physical world here? That is what I believe it to be. But my version of this is not what the mass population wants because it is not scary. Many of the old time Spiritualists believed that most ghostly occurrences seem to have happened with teenagers and usually young girls and they then took their opinions another even more bizarre step further by saying that these occurrences of ghostly events were somehow connected to the monthly hormonal cycles of these "high-strung" young girls. It amazes me how often things that cannot be explained by the limitations of the human brain at a particular time, are often the perception of an act of nature, a woman's menstrual cycle. Point of fact is that these people were just ignorant and based their opinions on the fears of their times and the need to find someone or something to blame and who is an easy target for that blame, young vulnerable hormonal girls.

We should always try to keep in mind that science and scientists have always had limitations because of the mindset and parameters they work and exist under. And as an aside, try to consider historically the eighteen fifties in the United States was the time that the suffragette movement was getting its footing to make its push through the Victorian era constraints which would also make sense as to why men might want to make the younger females feel confused and ashamed of the changes their bodies were going through. The repression caused by the male dominant society towards woman's bodies and its natural functions, had given birth to the need for Free Thinkers which is where the early Spiritualist built their foundation. Basically, men trying to hold women down under their thumbs created the atmosphere for the entire movement that Spiritualism and mediumship evolved from. There is an irony to the thought that the woman's suffragette movement was born at the same time as physical manifestations in western New York State to a couple of young "hormonal" girls, the Fox sisters.

This was the birth of modern. Spiritualism in the United States and physical mediumship may have been the step child of ideologies of repression.

9 "NEVER LET ANOTHER'S OPINION BECOME YOUR REALITY"
-LES BROWN

Once in conversation with a fellow student of mediumship we were discussing the fact that I had an evening planned where I would be doing seven thirty minute readings in a row. Another very opinionated student medium who overheard our conversation blurted, "You can't hold your energy for that long". I remember being immediately annoyed at her ill-informed opinion but instead of getting angry, I turned and asked her this, "How could you possibly know how long I can hold my energy when I don't even know at this point how long I can hold my energy?" As a student at that stage of development if I were to buy into her version of my reality regarding my energy I might have believed her and not done well for my seven sitters that next night. The reality was that I was able to hold my energy for all seven readings and the last reading was just as evidential and helpful as the first reading. So she was wrong and it taught me a great lesson about owning my mediumship.

To become a credible medium working for the highest good of all involved, there is a level of commitment and ownership that is as intimate and personal as any human relationship you will ever have. Spirit wants us to do well and will do amazing things to help our development as mediums. For myself I have found that with the amount of time that I spend connected to and working for spirit it has become one of the most important and rewarding relationships

I have ever had. Yes I said a relationship. I live my life as a medium considering my connection to spirit to be a relationship I am participating in. Just as you would treat any human relationship you are involved in you might check in during the day to see how they are or think about them during the course of your day just as you would for a friend or loved one. That is how I am involved with spirit. I am in a loving relationship with spirit as a whole and not any specific spirit. I find myself drifting to thoughts of spirit while waiting on lines in stores or while I am driving. I absolutely love being in a relationship with spirit and I feel a sense of unconditional love back from spirit as well. Not in a romantic way but more as that of an old friend that would always be there for you supportive and accepting no matter what the situation. Do I consider spirit to be my best friend? No, but I do consider spirit to be my closest friend, and there is a trust that has been built between us that I value as much if not more than some relationships I have here in the physical world. I look forward to growing old with spirit and reconnecting again after I leave this physical world when my work is done here.

Often after hearing that I am a medium I am asked by the curious person, was I born this way, or what happened? I used to laugh at this question but now I understand their natural curiosity. I may be the first person they have ever met who is able to speak to people who have passed over to the spirit side of life. My answer is always the same to them, yes I was born this way, and I believe all mediums are chosen by spirit before they are even born into the physical world. However what happened to me question, I will answer only if I have the time and inclination to share one of the most intimate moments in my life.

Whenever I am addressing a large group of an audience where I will be doing a public display of mediumship or smaller groups where I will be doing one to one private readings. I always remind them that there is absolutely nothing special about me in the process, there is however, something special I can do. By saying it in this way, it projects the humility with which I live and choose to approach my work for the spirit world. My ego needs to be held in check and I aspire to provide healing and meaningful readings that come from a place of love that will be for the highest good of all involved. Far too many times, and I have been guilty of this early in my unfoldment; the information brought forth in a client's reading has become more about look at what I did instead of staying out of the way and allowing this intimate moment happen between the spirit sending the message and the recipient receiving it. That is pure ego and attention seeking behavior at work and it serves no meaningful purpose for the communication between the two worlds.

It takes a strong self-knowledge and an understanding of the true reason spirit is working through you to move your ego out of the process. This is where many student mediums fail in their desire to serve spirit. They like the idea of doing it and the attention they receive from doing it but that becomes their driving force to their version of mediumship and it will never reach its highest potential. What a shame for them to have squandered the trust and opportunity brought forth by those in spirit. You have such a wonderful gift has been said to me many times by people who have touched my mediumship. The truth is yes it is a gift, but not in the way they perceive it. It is not a gift given to me, but more so a gift given to them from spirit. My role in all of this is to be an instrument that spirit uses for their purpose in that moment. I as the medium are responsible for making sure that my instrument is in the best working order for the needs of spirit, and I do that by living a spiritual life and continue working towards the betterment of my abilities as a working medium. I am an employee working for spirit and I understand the importance of my role in this relationship, and I am grateful and humbled by their trust in me.

10 "ELVIS HAS LEFT THE BUILDING"
-COL. TOM PARKER

As a medium giving a one to one reading for a sitter the aim is to bring through the loved ones of the person sitting across from you. What is the purpose of this "grand experiment"? To show proof of life continuing after the transition we call death? To bring anecdotal information so that the sitter believes that their loved one is still around this physical life even now after their transition to the spirit side of life? I believe that it is a more complex question than that, which is what it is thought to be. My take on what mind to mind spirit communication is all about has more to do with love than anything else. Yes, we love to receive messages about our beloveds in the afterlife and we do so need to feel connected to them, but my sense based on thousands of readings is that the real value in spirit communication is to prove that the bonds of love have not been severed or forgotten by the event of someone's natural death. What I mean by the term natural death is the physical body is no longer alive in this physical world on this planet we call Earth. That is a very simple explanation so that when I talk about someone's death or transition there is no question to what I mean.

I was trying to be a bit funny by quoting Colonel Tom Parker who was Elvis Presley's manager for most of his career. As a showman Col. Parker knew that it would build a better audience if you leave them want for more. While the young fans screamed for more songs by Elvis after he ended his show and left the stage, Col. Parker made it a point to never bring Elvis back for an encore. That is where the expression "Elvis has left the building" came from so that the fans knew the show was over. Period! I use this metaphor of some people's perception of what happens to us after we leave this physical world through our event of death. Some people believe that when you die you are just dead, gone, no longer existing, like Elvis you have left the building. My problem with that understanding comes in the facts that show me something differing from that view. Einstein and other physicists have shown through quantum physics that energy can never be totally destroyed. Since we are living breathing energy what happens to us after our organs no longer function and the physical body dies? We are more than the sum total of our organs we also possess a soul and a spirit. Our soul and our spirit are the true essence of who we are. Our connections of love live in them. Our personality traits and thoughts are to be found there. They were never imprisoned in the physical body that is capable of withering away. They are eternal and will always exist. Eternal is a two way street, we are eternal into the infinite future and we have been eternal in the infinite past. The only place that we truly exist in the physical world is in the here and now. Our limited time in the physical world is a small part of eternity.

"Everything science has taught me, and continues to teach me strengthens my belief in continuity of our spiritual existence after death. Nothing disappears without a trace". Wernher von Braun

All through the ages of man the question of what is a soul has been asked and answered in many various ways. Philosophers and theologians have been and probably will always debate what constitutes a soul. I am neither a philosopher nor a theologian but I will offer an opinion based on my limited expertise as a medium that lives a spiritual life communicating with those in spirit. I believe that all human beings have a soul. With that being stated up front I then bring your attention to that part of yourself that talks to you, your inner voice. Some think it to be their conscience but I think there is another deeper level to your inner voice that speaks to you from a place that is connected to all that has ever been and all that will ever be, your God, your Source, the One, whatever name you are comfortable calling this. This is your spark of Divinity that which came from the Source and returns Home to God when our physical life ends here on this planet. Your spark of divinity is called your higher self by some and this is where you go when you need the answers to the questions that come up during your life here on Earth.

You were born with the answers to every question that will come up in your life already inside of you. I do not state this as a belief but as a knowing. I know this to be a truth.

In an attempt to simplify an explanation of what our spirit is, it might be this. Picture a very long piece of rope, every now and then there is a knot in that rope. The rope seems to have no beginning and it seems to go on forever. Spirit is that rope and the knots are the time that you are in another existence even one possibly being your time in this particular physical life. I believe that your spirit has always been a part of you and will continue to always be a part of you. I do not know if we have other incarnations into this world or into other worlds. I don't believe that anyone can definitively prove that. I understand the idea of reincarnation as expressed in eastern religions; I'm just not sure if I truly buy into that belief system. Nothing in my mediumship has shown me anything that would corroborate the reoccurrence of our spirit into other physical bodies. Just as I do not believe when a television medium shouts to an audience member that their new child is really their grandfather come back. To me that is just silliness and grandstanding for sake of selling products on the commercial breaks of the television show. There is no sign of anything evidential about a claim like that and I can see no intelligence from the spirit side of life in a scenario like that. The alleged medium is not only not proving continuity of life but is actually proving that life can be ended by someone newly born taking the soul of your departed loved one. It is more than ludicrous it is unethical to tell someone that because it is a lie and a dangerous one at that. Be wary of public mediums making outlandish claims and saying it is coming from the spirit world. They have the ability to help people but they also have the ability to hurt people if they are not coming from the right place in their version of mediumship. I'm also of the belief that as a medium we own every word that comes out of our mouth while connected with spirit. This alleged medium will pass to the spirit side of life one day and now has to face that grandfather and explain why she or he lied to their loved ones. That is karma truly at work!

At the very least a medium should always come from a place of respect when working for the spirit world. Remember- first do no harm! If the medium were to adhere to the golden rule that is found in one context or another in just about every religion that has ever been in existence on this planet, they would not do anything to anyone that they wouldn't want done to themselves. If a medium cannot be helpful, than at the least they should not be harmful. I struggle in my own mind even referring to these people as mediums as I don't think they are truly working for the good of all involved but from a place of what is good for the bottom line of their own pockets. That is not what mediumship is meant to be.

Most working mediums will never become rich from this type of work. About eighty percent of practicing mediums make almost no income from their mediumship efforts. They rarely even cover their own expenses for their studies and developmental circles. About fifteen percent make enough money from their mediumship to cover their expenses but probably see very little profit. Of the approximate five percent who are able to pay their expenses from their mediumship maybe two percent make as much or more than the average teacher in a public school. If you think becoming a medium is a road to wealth you are wildly misinformed. I have even had conversations with working mediums that are living on public assistance and using food stamps to help provide for their survival. Most working mediums must have another "legit" job to help with their day to day living expenses. I am aware of incredibly gifted mediums in places like Lily Dale that work in the off season at Home Depot or Wal-Mart. In the pre WWII days in England, the mediums believed that spirit would take care of their needs and somehow they always made their monthly bills. But having read literally scores of books about those same mediums, not one of them became wealthy while in the service of the spirit world.

Mediums choose to do this type of work because it is a calling. It is somehow given to you and there is an opportunity to spend your life in service to your fellow man and for the higher good of all people. That is why I chose to work with spirit and it seems to be the reason most credible mediums I know have chosen to work for spirit. This is also another place to show the importance of free will in our lives. Here in the United States I have a friend who is a wonderful medium, trained as a corporate executive and had earned a nice comfortable six figure income for many years, yet she chose to leave that life and lifestyle because she wanted to spend the rest of her life helping others who struggle. I have met so many mediums with similar stories that it makes my heart smile to know that this level of humanity exists during this difficult time in history. This is the goodness of people, this is what I believe is important in life. Not the bigger house or the corner office at work but to know that you make an impact on people's lives and they are better off for having known you if only for that brief reading. It allows them to touch the higher side of humanity and that can be a transformative moment in that person's life. That is when we are living the meaningful life that is part of the shared community of this time at this place and we have chosen to engage life and not to just be a spectator.

As a working medium who has to work at another line of work when not practicing my mediumship I find it hard to understand why someone would balk at paying the price for a reading. If you truly cannot afford a reading but are in dire need for one I do not know of any medium that would turn you away. If you can afford the price of a reading try not to insult the medium by looking to dicker or haggle over the fee. You may in that moment win a small victory but you have no idea of how much time and effort that medium has put into their development so that you could be a participant in a small miracle. That is how I see mind to mind spirit communication to be, a small miracle and I believe all miracles are small at some point. What price would you place on a chance to hear from someone you love and have lost to their passing into spirit? Mediums place a value on their readings based on how they perceive the value of their gift of mediumship. How could you possibly determine that value before you have even sat and had a reading?

I had an experience once where I was asked to come to a home to do readings for a group of six related people. Before I even arrived to that house the hostess had put pressure on me to lower my price for her group. I was naïve and lowered my price on her claims of financial hardships for her and her group. I went through with the readings and all were happy with their readings. But I was unhappy with myself afterwards. The house that I had gone to for these readings was worth over a million dollars, three times the value of my home at that time. Each of my alleged indigent sitters were either corporate types or married to corporate types earning more than five times my annual income at that point by my guesses. I had been hustled by people of means who truly could afford my services but did not value them the same way I did. In the end these people were poor but not in a financial way but in their choices and judgments. Spirit taught me a valuable lesson that night and I have never forgotten it. I am in charge of the value of my mediumship and my readings. Needless to say I never mentioned this to any of her friends as I was a frequent evening's entertainment in that part of the county I lived in. But there is a piece of me that wanted to say shame on you for lying to me, because at that very same time my own home was in foreclosure and I was struggling to pay my share of my child's college education. If I were to come from a place of ego I would say that I would never read for that group again, but that is not what I would do. If there were a need for a reading and I could help relieve some pain or anguish from their life, I would do the reading. I would however expect to be paid the rate that I have set and it would not be open to negotiation. Spirit has not given me the task of punishing these souls for their insensitivity, but rather the task to show them love in spite of their insensitivity.

I am a true believer in the words love is always the answer. No matter what the situation, if there is an opportunity to bring love into it I think you should try your hardest to bring the love. It may be the single most important thing that a human being can do, to come from a place of love even in a most difficult place. This is what I believe our higher self would want us to do. It is not always easy to do but most of the time I have found, the easy way is hardly the best way. I am human and my feelings can be hurt, but I am the one who has the free will to choose whether to stay hurt by carrying it along with me, or to let it go therefore taking back my power in that situation. I much prefer climbing my mountain without someone else's baggage on my back. Who knows? If you are someone who believes that we have had past lives maybe I had cheated someone in another scenario and this was karmic payback for that past encounter. I am inclined to believe that some people just need to have gotten the better deal over someone else no matter what the situation, even in paying less for their participation in a small miracle. Was this one of my life lessons? I don't know, but I did learn from it and for that I am grateful.

11 "NO ONE CAN GIVE YOU WISER ADVICE THAN YOURSELF" -CICERO

If a person lives to be eighty years old that means they will have been alive in the physical world for approximately twenty nine thousand and two hundred days. That seems to be a lot of days. What I have noticed as a medium is that for some reason we seem to be very interested in the very last day of a person's life, the day of the event of their passing into the world of spirit. Many times in readings the spirit loved ones will come back with messages about the life they led and the shared memories they had while still in the living. They will often touch upon how they passed and many times they will even share the actual event of their passing with me so that I may understand complete version of their story here in the physical. I am always appreciative of that very intimate sharing. But many times our spirit beloveds also make a point that the people they left behind here in the physical world are too caught up in the drama of the day of their death. It is almost as if they are saying they wish we would pay just as much attention to the other twenty nine thousand one hundred and ninety nine days that I was with you in the physical world. We tend to think of their event of passing as what defines them when in reality there was and is so much more to their story than just that last day on Earth.

I went through a period in my development as a medium where those in spirit would share a visual with me of the event of their death. I have now worked it out with spirit that they can tell me about their passing or show me if it is absolutely necessary as I was having too many visuals of difficult dying events especially those that passed in accidents or by violent means whether self-inflicted or otherwise. They can stay with you and it does take time for me to process that type of visual.

I was called to do a reading for a gentleman and when I met with him I immediately connected with a young man who let me know that he had passed in horrific car accident. I assumed it was this man's son but it turned out to be his nephew that he raised in the role of a second father. I could understand how I could mistake that type of energy since they did live in the same house and he was active in raising this young man. Prior to me going to meet this man for this reading I felt this young man's energy while I was getting ready and taking a shower. I often a get a download of information before the actual reading and many times it can happen while I have my head back rinsing in the shower. I kept hearing this young person saying memorize this, memorize this, so I did and I wrote down what I thought he said to me while I was showering when I got to a pen and paper. I wrote the words phonetically as I had thought I heard them. I stuck that piece of paper in my back pocket of the pants I was going to be wearing that day. As I now sat with this uncle who was in a deep state of grief, his nephew came through as an incredible communicator from spirit.

I explained to the uncle that this young man named Nick was showing me that he had been driving on a rainy and very foggy night and he pulled his car over to the inside shoulder of a six lane highway. As he walked around his car, for a reason I am not aware of he was struck by a speeding vehicle. It was at this point that he impressed on me that he did not feel any pain and did not experience his passing in the way that his relatives believed he did. I shared that with his uncle. After being struck from the speeding car going south his body was thrown into the oncoming traffic of the northbound side of the highway and he was struck again. What he showed me at that point in a visual was that he left his body like a wisp of air instantaneously and never felt any of the accident. He was however, if I understood his impressions correctly a witness to this fatal accident that took his life. As I am describing this scene to his uncle the uncle confirmed that I was correct that his nephew was named Nick and that is the way this accident was portrayed in the police report by the accounts of the eye witnesses at the scene. As you can imagine this man was very upset as I recounted the version of what I had been shown. I reiterated what the spirit communicator had expressed to me that he never felt any pain that they may have thought he did and that his spirit left his body at the moment before the impact. As I was finishing up the reading and getting ready to shut off my cd recorder I remembered the little piece of paper in my back pocket and explained to the uncle how I came about having it. The words on the paper were "*jam shume lumptner*" this man with tears now falling from his eyes looked at me and asked me if I spoke Albanian? I told him no and that I'm barely coherent in English trying to lift his mood. He repeated the words over and over a few times and then he just broke down and sobbed. When he was able to continue he told me that even though I had spelled it a little wrong what his nephew was saying was "I am happy". This nephew had given this man a huge gift that day and it left me with a lump in my throat as well, and one of the more memorable readings I have done to date. Over the course of the next year I had the honor to bring that young man through for many other relatives of his and most importantly to his parents who initially were not interested in reconnecting with their son through the work of a medium. They were so fearful of meeting with a medium that they had me do their reading in the driveway at their house. They didn't want me to go inside their home, I guess in case

I left some spirits behind after I left. I did not take it personally and I abided their wishes and did not feel anything other than honored to be able to have served spirit for them that day and think of them from time to time and hope that they are able to find closure and take their son's memory with them as they move forward in their lives.

On another occasion while doing an evening of one to one private readings for a group of seven ladies in the home of a well-known doctor there came a time when I read for the hostess for the evening. Her mother had come through very nicely with evidence of her knowledge of the fact that this lady was the mother to five children, four boys and the last child the only girl and that her name is Cara. I was most happy with my communicator as she was making me look like a great medium while doing the work for spirit. I still had three more readings to do after this particular sitter and the spirit must have sensed that the reading was coming to a close. Out of nowhere I heard in my ear "*ick how jow van*" It threw me off a bit as I did not understand what I was mumbling. In a very gentle manner I was being told that I was saying it wrong so I took in a slow breath which is how I normally receive information. Slowly I said to this sitter "write this down phonetically, *ick how van jow*". She was just as puzzled as I was from what I was communicating to her from her mother. I felt the energy shift and I knew that I was dropping the link with this spirit lady. Just to clarify something you may have been wondering about. When a reading is finished it is not because the spirit has decided to leave or they get tired. I believe that the spirit would go on communicating endlessly, if allowed. It is the medium who may tire or drop the connection similar to a dropped call on your cellular phone. Sometimes the medium just has a feeling of when to stop a reading or they may be regulating their timing so that they can maintain the level of their mediumship for the rest of the evening's readings.

As my sitter was getting up to go back the common area that everyone had gathered to discuss and share their readings with each other, I asked her to let me know later if she can find out what "*ick how van jow*" means? I did the next three readings and came downstairs to finish the evening's work and collect my things to start my way home when I saw this woman just beaming. She said she went on the internet and typed in what I had said to her. She told me that her mother was originally from Holland and had passed when she was just a young girl and that even though she never had the opportunity to learn her mother's first language which was Dutch. "Ick hou van jou", a corrected spelling and not the phonetic one that I had given actually meant "I love you" in Dutch. This mother had come through with something that I would have no way of knowing just to tell her little girl that she loves her one more time. I was moved by how wonderful gift the spirit mother had brought to her daughter and this was profound for this daughter. I am ever so grateful and in awe of the power of love even after one had left the physical world. I will remember that reading forever. This individual reading just adds to my understanding of how mind to mind communication truly is based on the bonds of love between two worlds. If you ever need to wonder why a credible medium labors so long and so hard, to be a participant in a sharing of continued love from the spirit world to the physical world is reward in itself and I am ever so grateful to have touched that energy.

While working in a class at the Arthur Findlay College at Stansted Hall in England I was paired with a beautiful woman from The Netherlands. The exercise that we were to given to do was to get a spirit person belonging to our partner. She did a wonderful job for me bringing through an aunt from my mother's family who treated me most kindly when I was a small boy and it was great to connect with her again these many years later. As I gently blended with spirit I immediately felt the presence of a younger male and I knew that he had passed after a lengthy illness and it felt like a cancer condition, but I could not get a sense of which cancer this spirit had passed from. Many times the spirit communicator will tell you very specific information about their medical reasons for their lives ending, but not in this case, I just knew that it was cancer that took him to spirit. I sensed that this young man had a romantic connection to this woman at one point in their lives. He shared with me certain films that they had seen together which she later confirmed. I connected the name of Peter to him but was not sure if that was his name or someone they both knew. I mentioned to her that he was drawing my attention to his eyes and I interpreted that he must have had strikingly beautiful eyes. She started to cry but I stayed in my connection to him in spirit. I knew that if I stopped to attend to her emotions at that moment I might not be able to maintain this wonderful link that I was having with this young man in spirit. He showed me what looked like someone taking their driving license test. I told her what I was seeing thinking that he may have took her to her driving test or taught her how to drive I wasn't sure how to interpret this visual that I was enjoying. She was becoming more emotional and I felt my energy shift from the spirit world back into the classroom which was actually the magnificent chapel at Stansted Hall.

As I comforted her and a friend passed her some tissues she started to thank me for what I had done, I was somewhat startled by her response to the reading as this was pretty early on in my development and honestly, I didn't realize the impact of a reading that strongly before. She then went onto to share with me that this was an old boyfriend of hers and that even after they had no longer been a romantic couple they had stayed close friends. She even went on to say that this young man even introduced her to her husband and they all were part of a very close knit group of friends. I remember thinking to myself that how cool that was to all stay friends after a split up. She proceeded to tell me that he did indeed come down with cancer, a brain tumor to be precise that was malignant and had caused him to lose his eyesight. He was blind for that last two years of his life. So that explained why he wanted me to mention his eyes, it wasn't because of how beautiful they were as was my interpretation but that he actually could not see out of them anymore. This is one of those moments where you realize that what spirit shares with us is always correct but me the medium can misinterpret what I am receiving. I am human and I know that interpretations get more precise and finely honed with more experience. She continued on with her explanation of her friend and his story.

She told me that I was close on his name. It was not Peter, but I believe she said it was Peer. I'm going on memory here and I think that was about as close as I could get to a name like Peter. I had not known of the name Peer so I didn't have it in my repertory for spirit to draw from. She started to choke up again as she tried to speak and I held her hand to comfort her. She said that a few months before he passed she took him to a desolate area by car and she let him drive her car. She said that it was the last wish that he had was to drive a car one more time even though he was totally blind by this point in his illness. She told the story and soon we were both laughing as she explained how she would yell him to steer left, left..., no slow down! Brake! To the right! She said it was most happy day for him and one of the last good days he would have before slipping into a coma a couple of weeks after his final drive. He passed to spirit while still in that coma. She couldn't believe that he had come back and brought that story with him. Because of the level of compassion and intimacy that came through in her reading she and I became friends. Even though she lives in Europe and I in New York we still stay in touch and I value her friendship and will never forget her friend Peer.

Interestingly enough, in a note that she had sent me about a year after that reading, she signed the note with, "ik hou van jou". I love you. One of the many benefits of training at the Arthur Findlay College is that you get to work with mediums from all over the world. It is an incredibly humbling experience to see the amount of love and hard work that is happening not just where I live but in the rest of the world on the behalf of service to the spirit world. This may be part of the reason that most mediums seem hopeful when you meet them. They may have an awareness that things are going to be alright in the long run for the human race. This may also help to explain why people are drawn to a medium; I often think there is more to this than just spirit connections. It may be that sense of life affirming hope that this difficult place we live in will be okay when a person connects to a medium. I also know that everybody has a million questions when they get to meet a medium, and I welcome the chance to share what I know with them.

12 "WE WILL FOREVER BE KNOWN BY THE TRACKS WE LEAVE BEHIND" - DAKOTA

Early on in my own development in mediumship I felt a presence outside of myself but inexplicably connected to me. Since that first experience, I have felt that type of connection a few more times. Some I still feel connected to while with others I don't feel their energy around me any longer. My understanding of those phenomena is that they may be my spirit guides or what some people like to call my guardian angels. I struggle with either of those terms and I'm not sure why. To be honest, I am still very skeptical of things that I cannot wrap my head around fully.

As I sat and meditated one beautiful spring day, with my eyes closed, I felt the presence of someone or something sort of around me but not in a way that made me think I was threatened or in any way in danger. It felt more like an old friend or like I was sitting with an old relative. That is the best way that I can explain in words how this relationship felt. I visualized a short man who looked to be like an Inuit Indian or an Eskimo. His features were very similar to that of those who live amongst those tribes. His hair was black and his bangs were very short, riding up near his hairline and choppy looking. He was dressed warmly and had a genuine warmth and kindness in his face and demeanor. I have felt his presence thousands of times since that first encounter, and I have always felt a sense of love from him and from me towards him as well. When I asked him for a name, I heard Aki, not from his lips but in a mind to mind transfer of thought. I believe now that he has been my main spirit guide and someone who has known me far longer than my understanding of knowing myself.

A week or so earlier I had felt another presence and it was that of a man who looked like a lumberjack, only much smaller in stature. He had reddish hair that was mostly hidden by a woolen cap that has changed colors at different times that I have felt him nearby. I believe that he was Canadian and he gave the name Jean Paul, the name I have come to use when I feel him around me. He always seems to be very happy and quite jovial in nature, I have never gotten a sense of what his role or his connection to me is, however, I still like being connected to him.

I have also felt the presence of a Middle Eastern woman who has given me the name Miriam as a way of recognizing her. She has dark almond shaped eyes and long wavy thick dark hair. Her facial complexion is a bit rough as if she had some skin issue at some point. Her energy always feels very loving towards me and I welcome her anytime I notice her presence nearby. I have also felt the presence of on older Asian man who appears to be of Japanese heritage. He is the least vocal of all of these visitors I have come to know. When I asked him for a name I was told that any names that I may be given are for me so I understand the different energies that will work with me, but that the names are not real to them. Nor is it important that they even have names. The name that I have come to know him by is Mr. Soto.

I know from having read all of the Silver Birch books, in which Silver Birch was described by Maurice Barbanell as a "Native American Red Indian" but reveals himself to actually be of Egyptian origin and not Native American, that spirit guides may present themselves how they think we can best accept them For more than forty years, Barbanell brought through tremendous works of philosophy from Silver Birch. When questioned as to why he appeared different than what he was, Silver Birch's reply was that it was for the instrument to understand him better, the instrument being the trance communicator Maurice Barbanell. I have come to understand that these new energies in my life are actually not new to me, and may have been with me far longer than I can understand at this stage of my spiritual development. More importantly for me, they may not even be who or what I believe them to be.

As weeks went by and I became more and more aware of their presences and became accustomed to feeling them around me I just accepted that they were there and really didn't pay too much attention to them. While sitting at my computer one day I decided to Google the names of my new friends. Jean Paul I didn't Google as I figured he was just sort of the good time Charley personality and I'm not even sure what his purpose is. Once when after describing Jean Paul to a friend of mine she laughingly suggested that maybe Jean Paul was just a drunken spirit who saw an open window and fell in. I'm sure he has more purpose than that but I did enjoy the joke of her visual and I think Jean Paul did as well. When I looked up the name Aki it turned out that in Egyptian the work aki means brother. I thought that was pretty cool. The name Miriam in Egyptian means beloved love which I also found to be quite sweet and wonderful. When I looked up the name Soto in Japanese it turned out that there is a religious sect called the Soto whose main responsibility has to do with the subject of death. Wow, how appropriate for a medium whose main work is to deal with spirits who have gone through the process we call death. What I have come to understand since those early days of my development is that we may actually have a team of people on the otherside who work for us to help us along our journey in this physical world. Can they be like guardian angels? I'm not sure. I just know that they seem to be there and they don't seem to need to be acknowledged or named or ethnically typed in any way to work with us. I think they show themselves in those ways just so we humans can understand their presences.

While in another class at Stansted, I had the great fortune to have the opportunity to work in pairs with a wonderfully gifted medium from Ireland who happened to also be a trained psychologist and a mother of five children. I was impressed that this woman with this incredibly busy life still took the time to work on her spirituality and her gifts of mediumship. The exercise we were to work on together was to go into a deeper state of meditation and meet and describe the spirit guide for our partner. I gave it an attempt and did rather poorly as I was still not a great meditator at that point of my development, but I did give it a good try. When it came time for my partner, she very easily connected to my spirit guide and described a Native American Indian that she described as looking like an Eskimo. She went on to say that I would know him by the name brother. This was Aki that she was meeting and describing and for me, this was affirmation of who my spirit guide was. I was so grateful to her for that reading. For me it was an amazing experience that I will never forget. As that exercise ended we had time for a chat and sat with a cup of tea. That lady, that day, changed my life forever, and for that I am eternally grateful for her.

We sat and had the most wonderful conversation mostly about our lives at that moment. I was not a stranger to therapy or psychotherapy, having gone for years. In that hour-long conversation that sweet woman got to the core of what was going on in my life, especially regarding a long term romantic relationship I was involved in. She was able to tap into something inside of me, and to this day I have to believe that when she touched into my guides, who I believe are connected to my higher self, she was able to see what the issues I was struggling with were. Even more importantly, she gave me a road map out of that dark place I had been living in, a most unhealthy relationship. I only saw this lady one other time on the grounds of the school and I went up to her and hugged her and told her that she was an angel walking this Earth and that I felt blessed that she changed my life forever that day. She did more in that hour long conversation than all the years of psychotherapy. I really do believe that we are meant to be where we are, when we are, for a reason; a purpose. There are truly no coincidences; there is synchronicity and there is always a way out of despair. I ended the unhealthy relationship within days and have never looked back. That Irish mother gave me a gift I will never forget and I hope that I will repay it forward many times in my life as a sign of respect to her and my guides, for their love, that brought me back into the light.

People who come to see a medium after they have lost their loved ones often have similar questions based on commonalities of their relationship to the person in spirit. Spouses will come and ask me if they will be with their partner for eternity when they pass over to the other side. I truly don't know the answer to that question. The romantic part of my personality would hope for reuniting for eternity with that special love, however, I have seen so many different types of scenarios when I connect to the spirit world that I cannot say definitively that that is the case. What I can say definitively is that when a departed spouse comes through in a reading for their loved one still here in the physical world that they often hope that their loved one will find a new love.   Remember back to when you were first in love and you were in that euphoric state where you couldn't breathe and you couldn't eat because you were just so over the moon in love at the moment. Now, if you have children, remember when your first child was born. Perhaps that was like no other love you had ever felt before and it felt ten thousand times stronger than any other love you had ever experienced. Now, just try to imagine taking that state of love and multiplying again by another ten thousand times. That is the state of love that I believe our departed loved ones live in perpetually. State of love is what I refer to as the state of grace that we experience after we have passed away to the spirit side of life. When I approach a reading for a sitter I always come from a place of love and that is partly why spirit is able to provide me with a wonderful connection for my sitters. My thoughts are that the more we are feeling loved, the closer we can be to our loved ones in spirit. Love is the bond we are connected by even after the transition we call death, and love is the state of grace our loved ones are in now.

I have never had a spirit show any signs of jealousy or possessiveness. Those are Earth bound human qualities that do not seem to travel with us when we go home to spirit. I have on occasions had sitters ask me if I see their spouses with anybody else on the other side, usually meaning ex-husbands or old boyfriends. I have never answered that type of question as I think it crosses ethical boundaries that I do not want to venture into. I am not your spy into the spirit world or your personal private detective looking to see if your loved ones are now involved with someone else. You need to work those issues out some other way, it is not in my job description and I really am uncomfortable being put into that position. I am in the business of bringing through evidential information that will show you that your loved ones are still continuing on their spiritual life.

I have seen couples together that come through for their children after both have passed but that does not mean they are necessarily traveling through eternity together. They may have just come together for the reading for all I know. Most of the times that I have connected to a child or a baby that has passed; there is always someone else with them, like a grandmother or great aunt or sometimes a grandfather. I have never seen children by themselves. That doesn't necessarily mean that the spirit that was that child is with that loved one forever, they may just be together for the reading to allay any concerns a sitter may have about a child being alone over there.

Once, when doing a reading for a young mom who had traveled a great distance for a reading with me, the first visual I received was quite different and simply glorious to see. I was born into a Catholic family, so much of my early life was spent going to church and Sunday school where I learned the basics of that religion, so, many times I will receive visuals from spirit and signs that are connected to my early religious upbringing. When I connected to spirit for this young mom I saw the Holy Mother carrying a very tiny infant girl who I could tell was severely physically challenged and was not where she should have been developmentally. I then felt this wonderful wave of love pass through my body and I then saw the Holy Mother turn and walk away with this very sick little baby. I looked at this young mom sitting across from me and told her the vision I had just been witness to and she confirmed that she did indeed lose a newborn that was very severely challenged. I then told her that I was seeing the number 28 flashing in my mind, but she did not understand what the significance of 28 was. I also told her that I was then seeing the front cover of the novel "To Kill a Mockingbird." She looked at me blankly and said she didn't understand what that meant. She said she liked the book when she was thirteen, but other than that she had no idea. I saw the cover of the book again and I saw the author's name, Harper Lee. I mentioned that to her and she said, "My baby's name is Harper." I'm always amazed at the lengths spirit will go to bring information that is meaningful to the sitter.

About a week later, I received an email from this young

mom thanking me for the reading and the comfort that she felt after we had met. She then went on to inform me that she now remembered why the number 28 was so significant. It was her baby's birthday. Her daughter Harper was born on April 28th and even more interesting was that she looked up Harper Lee and found that she was also born on April 28th. In the midst of the reading, this poor mom had forgotten her own daughter's birthday. Some mediums refer to this as sitter's amnesia. It can happen to any of us who are not used to touching that spirit energy. This is why I believe it is so important to record all private readings. The sitter is not always going to understand or fully comprehend everything the medium is saying to them at that moment and it is great to be able to listen to it over and over again. I sympathize with all sitters as I have not always been a great sitter myself, so I know how things can go astray in the moment of the reading.

I once had a reading with a very famous medium from Europe who had an incredible reputation for the quality of his mediumship readings. I had to meet him at a hotel out on Long Island, New York. I had only been opening up to spirit for a month or so at this point. I admit that I did not pay for this reading as his fee was five hundred dollars and I could never have afforded that at that point in my life. A friend paid as she was the one who set up the appointment in hopes that this medium would provide more information about her young son who had recently passed. She had already gone to this medium but felt she needed more and she was so desperate to hear from her son again, so I agreed to go on her behalf. She was someone with the means to afford numerous readings at this price and she was willing to take the chance that her son would come through to me in this reading.

Starting a few days before the scheduled appointment which was to be an evening appointment on a rainy Tuesday evening, every time I would think of seeing this man I would get a slight twinge in the muscles of my chest. I didn't associate it with anything connected to this medium, but rather thought that maybe I had pulled a muscle or something explainable like that. I was not thinking I was in any kind of danger as it was just a very slight, barely noticeable twinge.

I met him at this hotel and he explained to me a little about how he worked and a little about how he believed spirit communicated to those of us still in the physical world. He was a very nice and gracious man and I felt very safe and comfortable with him. The reading went very well and my friend's son ended up being the dominant communicator so I was feeling good about her spending her money; I felt she got what she was hoping for. When the reading was over this gentleman and I had a nice twenty minute conversation about what was happening to me and he was very encouraging towards me developing my mediumistic abilities. He thought I had started out a little further along than many people who started down the path of their unfoldment. As he shook my hand goodbye and closed the door behind me, I had a much stronger twinge of pain in the same area of my chest.

After turning over the tape that had the reading on it to my friend, I asked her for his email as I felt I needed to mention something about what I had felt when I shook his hand goodbye the night before. I wasn't sure if it was the right thing to do, but I would have been miserable and angry with myself if I did nothing and then heard bad news later. She only had the general email that went to his assistant. I sent an email explaining who I was and when I had my reading and where it took place. I talked about what I had felt whenever I thought of his name and how it became strongest when I shook hands with him. I hadn't heard back from his assistant, when about five days later I received a personal email from this medium himself. In his email he thanked me for my email and understood my concern about boundaries and whether or not I should make him aware of what I had experienced. He then went on to tell me that one of his clients the following day was a leading cardiologist in Manhattan and so he went in for a checkup based on my concern. He thanked me for having the strength to reach out to him and that he was on his way back to Europe the following day to have a procedure done on his heart. The cardiologist had found something that needed to be taken care of immediately. He thanked me again and I was so happy that I made the right decision and got passed my fear of appearing like a fool.

Recently, I found that I had downloaded that reading onto a friend's computer when she loaned me the computer while mine was in the shop being fixed. I listened to the reading I received that night from that pretty famous medium and I was totally blown away. I had not heard it in over four years and the quality of the information he brought through for me was spot on. I don't believe he missed on anything that he shared with me. Not only in the parts relating to my friend's child that had passed, but he actually gave me some incredible evidence connected to my family, including naming all of my father's brothers and my father was one of ten children with only three sisters. I have probably been read hundreds of times by many different mediums with varying degrees of skill and talents, but that reading stands out in my mind as the best reading I have ever received. More importantly to me than just the fact that he showed me proof of continuity of life beyond any doubt, the conversation that we had after the reading turned out to be the push I needed to take my new found gifts to a level where I could strive to bring through information and evidence at the level he worked.

In the end was he worth the price that he charged? Not

having paid the money myself I don't think I should be the one to answer that. I do know however that my friend believed it was the best one thousand dollars she spent, because of the comfort she received from that reading and the knowledge that her child was alright and not alone on the spirit side of life. Years later, having been developing my own mediumship, I would love to have a chat with that gentleman again. It was a life changing experience for me and I am so grateful to her for making it possible.

13 "IT TAKES BOTH SIDES TO BUILD A BRIDGE" -FREDRIK NAEL

Sometimes a sitter will come to a reading with a medium and they are angry with the person in spirit who has passed. They are not usually angry with their loved one in a rational way, but rather because they miss them so much, they are angry with them for leaving them. It does make the reading a bit more difficult because a medium is someone with heightened senses and will feel the anger from that person and it can limit the medium's ability to deliver a quality reading. I understand that there are stages to the grieving process as has been wonderfully shown to us by Dr. Elisabeth Kubler Ross through her career long study and writing on death and the dying. I know from my own practical experience of mediumship and conversations that I have had with other credible mediums, that the more joyful and filled with love that you are at the time of your reading, the better your reading will be. This is not a hard fast rule of thumb, but just an observation. I also understand that sometimes you are just so heartbroken and in deep grief that you cannot help yourself at that stage to be more joyful. You will still get a healing and meaningful reading.

Please try to be fair and reasonable with your medium when you go for a sitting. We truly do this work out of love and a desire to be of service to our fellow man and to spirit. Whatever has happened in your life is a part of your story and you should never try to take it out on the medium who did not give you what you wanted. I have mentioned this before, but it bears mentioning again. Spirit does not always give people what they want, but instead spirit gives people what they need, and that is where the trust in spirit is paramount. If you come away from a reading unhappy because that medium did a lousy job and did not bring you who you wanted, it is likely not the medium's fault. As long as the medium was serving spirit to the best of his abilities and coming from a place of love, then there may be an issue in your attitude and there may be a need for you to look at yourself at that time. Let me rephrase this. Do you believe that the medium woke up that morning and said to themselves, "I think I will go and screw up someone's reading today intentionally?" Do you see how silly that sounds? Again, if you do your homework and find the right medium, spirit will always take care of their end of the process. Be fair and understand that maybe the medium had an off day; we are humans, not machines. We are trying to facilitate a small miracle of communication between the two worlds. Any credible medium who values their professional reputation will offer to give you your money back or not charge you if the reading is not working. They should recognize that it is not working, stop the reading, and refund the money within the first five or ten minutes. Not everybody is a good fit for everybody else. It's no one's fault, it has to do with chemistry, just as it does in all relationships. That does not mean that the medium was not good at their job. They were operating from a place of integrity and, as the old timers would say, they did the right thing.

I have only had this happen to me a couple of times, and I did not charge the person and went so far as to give them the names of a couple of other mediums who I thought might be a better fit for them.

Professional working mediums who strive to do the best

work for all involved in the communications from spirit to the physical world will have already figured out a system of support and referrals of other professionals they trust. I have sent numerous people to my main teacher to get a reading as I thought I was either not the right medium for them or that I was too close to them and may have known too much of their story to give them the best reading. I have been asked by some if I can do a reading for one of my own relatives or close friends? The answer is simple, yes and no. Yes, I can give a reading to someone I know very well but my ethics make me lean towards steering them to another medium that I trust will treat them respectfully and give them the quality reading I would give to them. It's kind of like a surgeon operating on his own loved one; can he do the operation? Of course he is capable, but it is probably best for all if he doesn't perform the surgery, but rather refers his loved one to a colleague that he has full confidence in.

Each and every reading is different because the energies of the parts that make up the reading are changing with each new sitter and group of spirit communicators who come for them. If you were to have readings with ten different mediums you would find that you have ten very different readings with some similarities and possibly even a few commonalities as well. Every time a medium endeavors to communicate with those on the spirit side of life, it is a grand experiment, in my estimation, a small miracle that you get to participate in.

If you can show up to your reading with your heart wide open and with enthusiasm about having the reading, you will have brought the secret ingredient to any great reading, a higher vibration. Your energy will help to raise your medium's vibration, which will then help you to have those wow moments that we all want in our readings. You will be the perfect sitter in an imperfect process and spirit will thank you for your efforts by bringing through what you need, not what you thought you wanted. Trust in the small miracle!

As a medium, I am aware that sometimes when someone comes to have a reading and to connect to the otherside, that they may be nervous or even a bit afraid. I promise you that there is nothing at all to be afraid of except maybe your own active imagination. Our loved ones in the spirit world would never hurt us or even think of hurting us. They exist in a state of love and bliss. On top of all of that, they are not even capable of hurting us as they are not in a physical body any longer. You have more to fear from people walking the Earth than you will ever have to fear with those in the spirit side of life. I know I have said this before and it bears repeating: you are perfectly safe and absolutely no harm will come to you when receiving a connection from the spirit world.

Try to think in a logical manner when considering having a spiritual reading done for you. Millions of people have had readings before you and nothing horrific ever happened to them, so why would you be the first to have a bizarre experience in a reading? It is like deciding to not have a baby because you don't know what could happen. Billions of babies have been born down through thousands of years so it is safe to say, it's probably going to be okay for you as well. Let's say that something totally horrible happened during a reading, what are the odds that it wouldn't be front page news or the lead story on the national news that evening. The media would have a feeding frenzy on a story of that magnitude. It's never going to happen, because spirit comes from a place of love and not from a place of fear. The absolute worst thing you might ever hear about a mediumship reading would likely concern one of the celebrity mediums being debunked as fraudulent for using sneaky video editing techniques or planting audience members so they look brilliant to millions. I'm sure it has happened and I'm sure they have been caught in the past. That is not true mediumship anyways. What I am talking about is you deciding to have a one to one reading with a credible legitimate, thoroughly tested medium who comes from a place of integrity.

Unrealistic expectations are sometimes what drives the nervousness of a sitter before a reading. I am a medium and this is what I CAN do: I can connect with your loved ones on the otherside and bring through enough evidential information so that you know that your loved ones still exist somewhere other than here and that they still love you and miss you as well. I am a medium and this is what I CANNOT do: I cannot make your departed loved one come back to life in any physical form, I cannot levitate or fly around the room and do weird things, I cannot leave a portal open to the other world so that bad spirits can come down and haunt you. None of these things are based in reality. They are things that the movie and television industries have created to sell tickets in theaters or to sell products during commercial breaks in television shows. None of what they do has anything to do with mind to mind communication from the spirit side of life to us here in the physical world. I know that I have addressed this before, but there are so many times I am asked questions like these or receive emails relating to incidences of alleged other-worldly activities. I hope this is the last time I answer something like that but my gut tells me, it won't be!

Many people in the world of psychics and mediums consider an Englishman named Gordon Higginson to have been the most gifted medium. His abilities were very broad based and he was able to serve spirit at such a higher level than just about anyone else who has ever done this work. There have been some amazingly talented mediums who were truly specialists of one type of phenomena, but Gordon Higginson was most proficient at many different types of mediumistic modalities such as mediumship, trance, physical mediumship and others. To truly understand the pathway of mediumship one would need to study the notable British mediums of the last one hundred years. The reason I am mentioning Mr. Higginson at this point is to share a story that one of the teachers from The Arthur Findlay College, Paul Jacobs, shared with us students. Paul complained once to Gordon that he didn't want to deal with some whiney client who was there to be read for what was going on in his life, rather than for a connection to the spirit world. According to Paul, Gordon slapped his face and reprimanded him for judging another person's sense of loss and need. Gordon believed that loss was loss and a man losing his job or a couple losing their home were just as entitled to help from a medium as someone who has lost a loved one. Paul said he never forgot that lesson and that Gordon was one hundred percent right. If you are truly interested in learning more about the best of the best in mediumship, I would suggest the biography of Gordon Higginson as a fine place to start.

In the back of this book I have listed books that I think would be interesting for anyone searching for a deeper learning of all things related to mediumship and Spiritualism. I have found a great respect for many of the pioneer mediums after reading about the sacrifices and struggles they had to endure to practice their religion and their gifts. Most of them made little to no money from their skills, but they chose to do this work out of a desire to serve spirit and fellow human beings who were in need. To me, these people were heroes in the truest sense of the word; selfless.

14 "THE DREAM CROSSED TWILIGHT, BETWEEN BIRTH AND DYING" – T.S. ELIOT

Many times I'm called to doing private readings in someone's home. There are times however that the reading will be something more than just a mind to mind communication between the two worlds. Sometimes it's a chance to meet with someone who is near the end of their life in the physical world. I'm not sure how this works to be honest with you , I just know that at times I have been able to meet with someone in the dying process and see what the event of their death will be like. I'm also not sure how other mediums handle a request to meet with a family at this point, but I always welcome the opportunity to do what I can in an honest way to help lift some of the fear that may surround the person who is dying. I have only done this a handful of times but for me as a medium, it felt like a true soul to soul connection experience and I am so honored to have participated in them.

I have learned with a sense of discipline to see the rooms in people's homes without actually looking at details of anything in particular. I do this out of a desire to not pick up any information about them or their loved ones from the pictures on the walls or the notes on the refrigerator. I noticed that when I first started to do readings at clients' homes that I couldn't help but be drawn to the cute pictures of the grandchildren on the refrigerators or the little trophies that one would accumulate while living a full life. I'm amazed now how I can sit in a room and not notice things anymore, it's sort of like the expression, can't see the trees for the forest. I've trained myself to be aware that I am in a forest but not to pay any attention to any of the trees with my conscious waking eyes. With this self-taught discipline I have discovered that when I close my eyes for a reading my third eye or clairvoyance ability has heightened. I will see details not only of the sitter's life, but also of their loved ones. I don't usually have travelling clairvoyance, an ability I know some mediums do have. On occasion I will get a picture in my mind of a room and then I can describe it pretty well and with accuracy that always amazes me.

There is a visual that I often get in private readings that is usually reserved for the scene of someone's passing that has been ill for an extended time. Many times I will see what some would call their death bed. I don't think of it that way. To me, many times it is a hospital bed, and sometimes it is a bed in their home, and even then it's a hospital bed that has been brought to the home in hopes of making the person more comfortable in their last days. Whenever I have had the honor to be shown the loved ones actually passing, I always treat it with respect and reverence, for to me, it is the most intimate and personal time in a person's life. I hope I never get to a place where sharing their death scene with me becomes a mundane or non-event. It is a sacred time in a person's life.

Tom was the love of Nancy's life. They were, in a way, dinosaurs in today's world in that they were junior high school sweethearts who never really had other relationships. Part of me is envious of that strength of a connection but there is another part of me that is happy that I have had the benefit of knowing other relationships. Tom was just 49 years old when they were told that his pancreatic cancer was no longer treatable and that he should get his life in order. Nancy did everything she could to make Tom's final days as comfortable as possible. She took care of him as if she was a nurse with forty years' experience. Nancy and Tom had two daughters, Melissa and Denise whom they called Missy and Niecy. These two young women, alongside their mom, provided Tom with one of the nicest death experiences I have ever had the privilege to encounter. Missy was pregnant with her first child and she knew it would be a male child. Tom made a promise to her that he would hold his first grandchild before anything would happen to him. As time grew nearer to her due date, Tom suddenly started to feel better. If you understand the death process, it is not unusual for a period of lucidity or what almost looks like a remission to occur. It is usually neither, but rather just another step closer to the final moments here on this side of life. Niecy is a young entrepreneur who started her own internet-based business and was doing quite well for a twenty-four year old. She found me through a good friend of hers whom I had done a reading for. Tom and Nancy were reluctant at first to have a medium come to their home to discuss death but after a persistent argument from their youngest daughter they acquiesced and I was called to come see the family.

For me as a medium, it is not just about providing information from the other side but also about bringing comfort and love into some of life's most difficult situations. Having visited people near the end of their time on this Earth, I have always found it to be quite humbling and incredibly honorable to sit with someone who doesn't have much more time here. I do appreciate that they would choose to share some of their most valuable time with me. I had said my prayers to my beloved spirit workers to help me find the right words to bring some sense of comfort to this family as their greatest personal drama was unfolding.

Upon entering Tom and Nancy's home I couldn't help but feel the love that was in the air. As I met each of these remarkable women I gave them a long and meaningful hug. With Missy it was almost a hug from afar as she was truly ready to have that little baby boy at any moment. Nancy put me right at ease by remarking as she pointed to Missy, "Is that the biggest gift you've ever seen?" As I sat with these three incredibly strong women sipping tea while Tom napped in his room which now was the living room with a hospital bed in the center of it. Hospice had been very helpful and kind with this family and they were so grateful and amazed that there were so many kind and wonderful people around helping people like them. From my own limited experience I have found hospice nurses to be some of the everyday angels walking this Earth. I sat there and listened to them talk about Tom with all of the stories of things he did for them and how he was always there for them no matter what was going on. He always made his girls his first priority. And when I say his girls, I am definitely including Nancy in that group. Not only were they madly in love with each other still after all those years together, but they were truly best friends as well. For a moment, I turned the sound of their conversation down in my mind and I started to get some visuals about Tom's passing. His time was coming to an end. I knew just sitting there on this Sunday afternoon that this would be the only time I would have to meet with Tom.

Nancy came back from checking on Tom and said, "He's up, would you like to meet Tom?" I smiled at her and went into their makeshift hospital living room. Tom reached out his shaking hand and I took it in mine and just told him how wonderful his girls were and how well they had been speaking of him. He motioned for me to sit beside him. I immediately liked Tom when he said to me, "Well, if you're seeing me right now does that mean I'm already dead?" I was a little shaken by his question, but when they all burst out laughing I knew this was a great man who had accepted his fate. We sat and talked like we had been friends forever even though we had only met minutes before. I told Tom that if he would like, I could try to give him an idea of how things might go for him. Again he made us all laugh when he said, "Well, yeah, of course, I need to know how the rest of the movie goes since I already know the ending." Out of the corner of my eye, I saw Nancy wipe away a tear.

I told Tom to relax and I felt myself connect to Spirit and I saw numerous people coming forward in my mind's eye. They were loved ones belonging to both Tom and Nancy. This is not always the most evidential type of mediumship, but I have found it to be, in my experience, as accurate as any other mediumship out there. I started to describe to Tom a woman who was his aunt and I felt that her name was Maryann or Marilyn who used to take him to the Bronx Zoo when he was just a little boy. Tom's eyes welled up and he asked, "Could it be my Aunt Marion? She used to take me there at least once a month when I was a kid." I went on to say that "There is an older gentleman here who is telling me that you were named after him and that he was a New York City cop when he was here." "Grandpa Tom!" he said with such joy in his voice. I then described a younger male who showed me that he had been playing near train tracks and was killed by a passing train that he couldn't get out of the way of fast enough. Tom said, "That's my friend Eddie Coughlin, he liked to play chicken with the trains and his luck just ran out one day and he lost the race." Tom looked very sad when remembering this event from his childhood.

Tom looked up at me and asked, "How are you seeing these people and why are they coming now?" This was the moment I had been waiting for. I said to him, "The reason they are coming now is because these are some of your loved ones who are coming to help take you over to the other side." Tom's eyes opened as wide as they could and he said, "You mean I'm going to see them all again? I thought they were dead." I went on to explain to Tom about how we can never die. We are energy and quantum physics has proven that energy can never be destroyed. I then tried to use an analogy that when we pass from this world to the next it may be similar to walking from one room through a doorway into another room. In the new room you see many of the people that mattered to you while you were on the Earth plane. In this new room there will be a window in which you will be able to see those that are still here. Tom looked at me and said, "You mean I'll still be able to be around my girls and the little guy?" pointing towards Missy. I said to Tom, "I promise you that you will always be around them when they need you to be or when you need to be around them." I also went on to explain to Tom some of the things I believed he would be doing once he went over. After a while I sensed that Tom was getting tired and it was time for me to leave. As I said my goodbyes Tom looked up at me and said "Thank you for taking away my fear, for the first time in my whole life I'm not afraid of dying." I thanked Tom for allowing me to share in the love that was in that home with that very special family.

I learned later that Missy went into labor the next day and delivered a beautiful strapping nine pound baby boy they named Thomas after his grandfather. Tom held his grandson many times over the next few days, mostly while they both slept with a happy mom and grandmother sitting right there. The following Saturday I thought of Tom and felt him at the Bronx Zoo with his Aunt Marion. I got a call that Tom had passed on that Saturday while holding his sleeping grandson. Niecy told me through tears, that her dad was so peaceful and just fell asleep with a slight smile on his face. This was a man who may not have lived as long as he wanted to, but, I promise you, this was a man who was loved every day of his life.

I recently heard from a young sitter who after his reading started noticing that he was dreaming more and that his dreams were more lucid, meaning more detailed and vivid. He called me when he had a particular dream about his dad who had passed into spirit a few years back. This young man and his dad had a very close and loving relationship, though he was the youngest in a very large family and sometimes his behavior was less than admirable. He sometimes partied too much. He was not the life of the party, however, as he became obstinate and difficult after he drank too much, and it seems that when he did drink, he always drank too much. When I spoke with him about the latest dream that he was struggling with I asked him what had been going on in the last few days. He admitted that he was feeling a lot of pressure from work and he had a young child who added to sleeping issues that he had had for many years. So, he was binge drinking; drinking to excess and becoming more obnoxious to his very patient and loving wife. His issues were coming to a head inside his sleeping head.

As we chatted he started to see that maybe his dad was showing up at this point just to give him a little nudge that maybe he should take a look at what he was doing to himself and his beautiful young family. I did little in that conversation except to patiently listen to what he was saying and to bounce it back to him so that he could hear it in a different voice. I am not a trained counselor and never have professed to be, but I am a good listener. After all, I am trained to listen to those in spirit. I then addressed his sleeping habits which were problematic because he made dumb choices and had convinced himself that he could only sleep if he had a drink or two to settle him down for sleep. This was total nonsense, so I gave him some homework to work on.

I explained to him that you can pretty much make or break just about any habit in twenty one days. I'm not even sure where I had heard that but I did use this information in the fatherly advice I dispensed to him. Did you get what I just said? The "fatherly" advice. Yes, that was what this man needed at that moment. He needed his dad to tell him what to do. Am I his dad? No, and I was not even connected to his dad in spirit but as one human being to another I could see that sounding like a dad might be the key to helping him through his dilemma. I asked him to commit to not drinking at all by the end of the next three weeks. I suggested that he change the timing of his drinks for the first week, which he did. In the second week, his job was to only drink every other day, which he did. By the end of the third week he was sleeping better than his toddler. According to his wife, who called me after the three week habit experiment, I had given her back the sweet loving person that she fell in love with and that she married.

I graciously accepted her compliment but disowned any part of the success that he was having in his new lifestyle. He called me for help. I listened and suggested a possible way to affect change. He did the hard work and was the one worthy of her praise not me. I happen to run into this couple with their child a few months later in a shopping mall and we were able to catch up and chat over a cup of coffee while their baby slept in the stroller. This young man went on to tell me that not only was he having more lucid dreams but that he was now able to remember many more of them upon awakening. He had sought treatment for his alcohol abuses in a twelve step program and had found new friends there who were very supportive and nurturing in accepting him and his family into their extended family. He had been an agent for change in his own life and I was proud of him and told him so. You could tell just by looking at how happy this man was at that moment that he may have struggles in his life, as we all do, but he has found a new set of coping skills. You could tell that he would be alright and go onto live a fuller more loving life. His wife again tried to thank me and I just held her hand and accepted her gratitude even though I did little. All gratitude when this heartfelt deserves a landing spot, and I was good with that. This all started because his dad chose to give him a wakeup call in his dreams so that he would have the chance to exercise the free will that was available to him. Getting to know this family was a real joy for me.

Being a medium that lives a spiritual life means more than just making mind to mind connections, sometimes it means using one's psychic abilities. All mediums are psychic, but few psychics are mediums. Most people have some form of intuition. Women tend to be more intuitive than men, but not always. Mothers also seem to have a higher level of intuition. That's where the expressions a woman's intuition or a mother's intuition came from. They are real and are part of the mysterious intangibles in life. The expression "trust your gut" is based on the intuitive nature within all of us.

Many higher functioning psychics are able to work within the parameters of scrying with great success. Scrying is an old term that encompasses many different ways to ascertain information that can be of value to someone, whether it is the psychic or the client. One of the most famous scryers was Nostradamus. He was a seer and many of his predictions about future events have come true to varying degrees; he is one of the most studied psychics of all time. His preferred method of scrying was to use either a very polished shiny black stone or a blackened bowl filled with water. He would stare into these and alter his awareness ever so slightly and then make his predictions for his clients or about the future. His accuracy may be unmatched and still unfolding.

I have been fortunate in my life to have met two very wonderful psychic mediums who were both very successful using the method of dowsing. Dowsing can be done in various ways. Some dowsers use a pendulum that they can either use over a map or land searching for locations of minerals, water or sometimes even people that are missing. Other dowsers use a y shaped piece of wood or metal and feel vibration changes which they use to provide information for clients or to locate missing valuables. The most common form of dowsing is to use dowsing rods that one holds in their hands to gain information from the movements of these brass or copper rods that swivel in different directions while being held by the dowser. I am by no means an expert in any form of dowsing, but I do find myself drawn to it at this point in my development and I may be studying it more as things progress.

There is a wonderful medium in Lily Dale by the name of B .Anne Gehman. The story of her mediumship and the life she has led can be found in the very engaging book "The Priest and the Medium." I highly recommend that you read this book if you are interested in learning more about an incredibly talented medium who also was gifted with an amazing ability to dowse.

In the early nineteen-eighties I had tried to earn a living writing screenplays with hopes that one would get optioned and made into a film. I was approached by another writer who had an idea for a screenplay after he had read a book about the wonderful New Jersey psychic Dorothy Allison and also a book about a psychic from Holland named M.B. Dykshoorn. After reading the two books and having absolutely no knowledge of anything psychic or otherworldly I went and met with Mr. Dykshoorn as he was living in the Riverdale section of New York City at this point in his life and my home was only a twenty minute drive from him. My friend tried to meet with Ms. Allison but was not able to arrange a meeting with her.

I went to Mr. Dykshoorn's co-op in the upscale

neighborhood he lived in and was shown to a waiting room by his lovely wife. He was with another client at the time. According to the book about Mr. Dykshoorn, after World War Two there was a scrambling search for many of the great art works and other valuables that had been confiscated by the German soldiers under orders from Hitler. Hitler an artist himself had decided that the spoils of his war were going to be the accumulation of much of the great art works and valuables of Europe from past centuries. Much of the art work was stored in various places and far too much of it was destroyed as the war turned in the favor of the Allied Forces. I guess Hitler thought that if he couldn't keep them then he might as well destroy the art. If you know anything about the fine master painters of the last five hundred years or so many of them were of Dutch ancestry, including Rembrandt, and Ver Meer amongst others. Perhaps this made it personal for Mr. Dykshoorn.

Using his dowsing abilities with maps of various cities and then actually going on foot to certain towns and cities, Mr. Dykshoorn was able to locate many important valuables. In one particular story, Mr. Dykshoorn had sent crews into a building and it was searched thoroughly with nothing being found. He argued with the searching crew and convinced them to go back and search again; still they found nothing. He so trusted his abilities that he was able to convince them to go back in and rip up the floorboards and when they did they found quite a large cache of paintings. There are numerous stories of Mr. Dykshoorn taking investigators into fields and unearthing boxes of silver coins and other valuables, some dating back four hundred years. There are also stories of Mr. Dykshoorn locating the bodies of missing soldiers from both World War One and World War Two. Imagine the closure that those families received from his findings. Sadly, both Mr. Dykshoorn and his wife of 58 years perished in a fire in the apartment building they lived in for many years. He was buried with the piano wire dowsing rod he worked with for many years. If you ever find yourself questioning the value of dowsing, please remember Mr. Dykshoorn's abilities and his legacy.

My collaborator and I, sadly, were not able to sell the idea for a movie about psychics or mediums. I guess we were about ten years ahead of our time before the breakout movie "Ghost" and the movie "The Sixth Sense" opened the public's mind to the subject of continuity of life after death. I am however, very happy to have become acquaintances with Ms. Gehman and honored to have had a conversation and a reading with Mr. Dykshoorn.

As I am apt to comment fairly often, be open to the people you meet and the lessons that may be available to you in all circumstances. There are no coincidences in life. People come into our life for a reason, it is not just happenstance. If you never wonder why new people keep entering your life you may be travelling through your lifetime with blinders on. If you move the blinders away, you may find a much fuller lifetime for you. An optimist sees the glass as half full, a pessimist sees the glass as half empty, and a realist sees the glass as always full, half of liquid, half of oxygen. I use to illustrate that there is more than what we may initially believe. Open your mind to the possibilities that exist outside of your glass. Simply stated, the more you open your mind and eyes, the more you shall see!

15 "DEATH IS PART OF THE ACHIEVEMENT OF LIFE" -MOTHER TERESA

Instinctually we fight for every second of life. We fear change and the unknown so much, yet it is one of the few guarantees we possess in this physical life. I understand that change is difficult for most people, some more than others. What I struggle to comprehend is the fear of the unknown. For thousands of years mediums have been giving glimpses of the afterlife, so it is actually somewhat known, but we still have something inside of us that struggles to grasp onto it. It may be that there have been so many different descriptions of what is to become our next stop on our spiritual journey, that we need more than what we have heard or seen to remove this fear. Someone had to be the first to leave the safety of the cave when humans were new to this planet. What was the drive that got that person to take that leap of faith? Has humanity lost that drive? I don't think we have. I believe that as we became more intelligent we believed in as little change as possible. It doesn't have to be a bad thing, but it may have taken a little piece of our sense of wonder away from us.

I honestly believe that people in general only fear the afterlife because no one has come back from there to tell us about it. The closest we have come to this are the experiences of legitimate mediums and credible near death experiences. For the average person, that is not enough proof that we exist still after we leave our physical body. One day, and it is not all that far off in the future, our science will be able to explain this transition we call death. It is only since the nineteen-seventies that any person in science spoke up to start the conversation on the dying process. People like Drs. Elisabeth Kubler Ross and Raymond Moody and the writer David Kessler have been the gatekeepers to the secrets of the ages. This may sound very poetic of me, but the truth is there is no secret. We have always known that all people will die eventually and they always have and they probably always will. What is different now, and especially in the last twenty years, is how quantum physics can provide a baseline for the new debate of what happens to us after we die.

As medicine improves and more is understood about how our total body works, more insight will uncover what has always been lying just under the surface, out of reach of our minds so far. As we evolve and our brain is able to comprehend on a level that it is not able to at this stage of humankind, we will break through the veil between life and death. It is right there, yet we are not equipped to comprehend it with the brains we operate with at this time. Do not despair. As the old adage goes, we are "a work in progress." We will get there when we are meant to get there and not a moment sooner. I'm not sure which would be worse, never finding the secret to life after death or actually finding it prematurely and not understanding it and therefore missing it. As a people, we are only as smart as our least intelligent human being. It is a progression that drives evolution as a species. Until we can tip the scales in the favor of the knowing versus the unknowing, man will continue to struggle with the bigger questions and the bigger picture. We have all heard the old maxim, "God only gives us what we can handle," and there may be volumes of truths in those few words. Those who are enlightened may see more or understand more, and those who cannot may provide the balancing force that steadies our course to understanding the divine or that which all human beings seem to go back to when they are no longer in this physical life.

Where humans have often been mistaken is in their belief that right is might and that strength is better than weakness. If we are all part of one whole, than we may need to rethink our approach to humanity in general. I am not saying that we need to exist to the level of our lowest common denominator, what I am saying is that as we are all one and the same parts of a whole, it would make more sense to pick up that which is behind or below the line of tipping . How do we do this? There is only one way that seems probable to me, and that is through loving our fellow human beings as if they were ourselves. That is what has been the most common of truths throughout the history of humankind. For every major religion, including some that aren't even around any longer, the truth is, basically the Golden Rule. Do unto others as you would have them do unto you. Why? Because they are you, and you are them; there is no separation other than those constructed by weak men stealing power over others for the wrong reasons. Is this going to change? Yes, it is going to change, as all things continue to grow and evolve. When will it happen? I have no idea except to say not in the time that I am alive in this physical world. I, however, am responsible for my actions here and I choose to add my layers of loving my fellow human beings onto the scales that, eventually, sometime in our distant future, change. It may take fifty thousand years for humankind to get to that place. It may happen sooner, but I believe it is inevitable.

As a medium, I can hold a conversation with you using my voice and mouth forming the words formulated by my brain with the thoughts and nuances from my mind. I believe that at some point in the future of our evolutionary process we will no longer communicate with our fellow human beings vocally in the way I just described. I believe that all communication one day will be mind to mind thoughts between humans; very similar to what a medium does now with those in the spirit side of life, except I believe that the human mind to mind communication will be more natural and less interpreting as we mediums must do in our version of mind to mind communication. I think this will be a major turning point for mankind as there will have to be more trust between humans for this communication to happen and I think that is where only time can help to bring this about. Will I see this in my lifetime? I say yes but not in the way you understand me at the moment. If by lifetime you are defining that as the time spent here in the physical body, then no, I won't see that. However, since I believe that my lifetime has always been and will always be; with no beginning and no ending; eternal and part of the divine, then, yes, I see mind to mind communication happening in my lifetime. I live my life with a much wider vision than if I only thought of this physical world as being life. This is what I was touching on before, about taking the blinders off and seeing so much more.

Do I expect everyone reading this to accept these views and to live life according to this visionary master plan? Of course not; I am not a cultist in the making. This is just the way I see life and where I see the bigger picture heading. You are entitled to come up with your own version and I would welcome a chance to learn about it. The average person hardly spends anytime thinking about the ideas of "what ifs," and that is understandable. We are all struggling to make a living and feed our families. The day to day life is difficult enough for far too many people. I have the luxury and the propensity to wonder and allow my mind to look for other answers to questions. It doesn't mean that I am correct; it just means that I am thinking about it and have this forum to share my thoughts. You can do the same if you choose to.

In the last few pages I have been inviting you to engage in

the discussion of the future of mankind. That is the sole purpose, for me to express my personal views of where I believe this world is at in its current stage of development and to invite you to join the conversation. I have provided some food for thought and perhaps you will have a brighter more insightful version of where we are headed as a people. The better you do, the better we all do. If I help to raise you up, rather than tear you down, I have also raised myself up in you. We are all connected whether we like it or not. I believe that is what God had in mind when he breathed life into this grand experiment we call humanity. He gave us free will to determine our own fate and progress, how do you think we are doing at this point? I think we're getting there, slowly but surely. I sometimes think of this life as the trailer to the main feature movie, and I can't wait to see the whole picture!

I sat on my couch meditating one exceptionally cold winter's day and my meditations at that time of my development usually lasted for close to an hour. At about the half hour mark, I heard a strong knocking on my front door which is located in the room straight out from where I was sitting. I immediately got up and went to see who was knocking at my door; I wasn't expecting anyone. My dog, who was quite old by then, had her large furry body lying in front of the door and she was in a sound sleep. As I slid the door open, she slid along with the door and did not wake up. I looked outside and there was no one there. I thought it strange that Ginger would not start to bark when someone came to the door. The truth is, if you came within a block of our house she would start to bark. And there she lay in a sound sleep at my feet.

I closed the door and then it hit me, maybe someone in spirit was trying to get my attention. So in a gentle voice I said out loud, "Welcome. I don't know who you are but you are welcome here." I went back and sat down on the couch and closed my eyes and just relaxed and tried to feel love towards whoever was possibly with me now. My couch sits in the middle of the room with the back of it facing into our dining room. With my eyes closed I heard soft but physical footsteps walking around the back of the couch and coming around the side and stopping right in front of me. I remember being excited and not scared at all. I opened my eyes and in front of me was my father's face about two feet across in diameter and he looked like he did when I was about three or four years old. He said in his own voice, which I hadn't heard in more than fifteen years since he had passed to spirit, "Hi Ya Cowboy!" I immediately burst into tears and started sobbing very strongly. His vision disappeared in an instant. Cowboy is what he called me whenever he would first see me when I was a very little boy. I honestly didn't remember him calling me cowboy until that moment.

I cried for about fifteen minutes. It was the deepest, longest crying I had done in many, many years and I felt great afterwards. I truly don't understand why I cried so heavily, but afterwards I was mad at myself for my reaction that seemed to scare my father's spirit away. I now understand that I didn't scare him away. He came to show me that he was around me, and I felt a tremendous amount of love in those few seconds. It was just so overwhelming that my emotions were let out, like a dog when someone leaves the gate open. It was a very cleansing release of pure loving emotions and I will always appreciate his visit that day. I was at a low point in my life and my father came to comfort me and show me that everything was going to be okay. It was at that point that I decided to come out of the mediumship closet to my mother.

My mother was raised in the Catholic Church, so I assumed she would tell me that it wasn't him and that it was the work of the devil. Interestingly, when I told her about my experience and of the other things that were happening at that point, she surprised me by telling me that my father had also come to visit her once before. About six months after he passed away from a sudden heart attack, after a lengthy illness of emphysema, he appeared to her in her bedroom one day. She said she was sitting on the edge of her bed and something drew her attention to the doorway into her bedroom, and there stood my father. She said he looked at her, smiled, and then just faded away. She also found it to be a very emotional visit and also had a good cry for herself. I asked her why she had never shared this story and she said, "I didn't think you would ever believe me." We both laughed about our little secret visits. It made me happy to hear that my dad had come back to smile at his wife of forty-three years, the love bond still connected them to each other.

In a different conversation with my mother, I asked her if she was aware of anyone else in her family ever having any of the abilities that I was now experiencing. She could not think of anyone having any. I also had a conversation a couple of years later with my Aunt Mary on my father's side of the family asking her the same question and she had no knowledge of anyone in the Samoyedny side having any experiences similar to what I was then having.

As an interesting side note to my inquiries regarding both sides of my ancestries and the abilities to communicate with those in the spirit world, once when at The Museum of Natural History in New York City I stumbled upon the Samoyed Tribe exhibit in the Asian section of the museum. I already knew that our ancestors were from that tribe going back many centuries. What I learned that day was that they were a nomadic people who struggled to survive in the Outer Mongolia part of what is now Russia. One of the things that they are thought to be known for was shamanism. This may be the direct link for me to understanding more about the gifts that have become a big part of my life now. We all have projects that we aspire to, what some refer to as things on their bucket lists, meaning things to accomplish before we die. For me; learning more about the Samoyed Tribe and their connection to shamanism is on my bucket list.

One of the benefits of writing a book that connects you with your past is that you learn things that you hadn't known before. Members of the Samoyed Tribe lived in the northern most parts of Siberia, up near the Arctic Circle. They looked physically very much like Eskimos and had related religious practices. They looked like my spirit guide Aki! The more I learn, the more I want to know. This may be my next set of studies. I'm thinking Aki may be my connection to my heritage and shamanism.

16 "LOVE AND HAPPINESS"
-REV. AL GREEN

If there can be such a thing as a favorite type of reading for a medium to do, then, for me, it is the readings that bring a person to a place of healing, that tug most at my heartstrings. I firmly believe that all mediumship that is coming from a place of love and with a true spirit link has tremendous value. When I arrive to do a series of readings, one after the other, I can always tell by the time I am finished working for spirit which of those sitters received the most benefit from their reading. I also know that if the sitter is open hearted and of the mindset that they are connected with their loved ones on the spirit side of life there will be many gems for them to discover in their reading. This is another reason why I always record readings that I do for a sitter; so that they may listen to the reading over and over. Those who listen back do connect with much more than they initially believed in their reading. It is an amazing process to be a part of. I am blessed to touch this energy on a regular basis; truly blessed and very grateful.

I had the pleasure to be called to a home in the Pittsburgh, PA area. I was scheduled to do seven one to one readings in a row. All was going along very nicely when in came my next sitter who happened to be an older gentleman who was still a practicing physician in that area. As his reading proceeded with many of his relatives giving him loving supportive evidential messages, I felt a shift in my energy. I shared with him that I felt a young man with me who had passed in his late teens and that my spirit communicator repeated over and over, "Stop blaming yourself, there was nothing you could've done." He just sat there and looked blank. I then heard from the spirit, "My name is Charlie and I am so sorry for what I did, it had nothing to do with you, stop blaming yourself." At that point my sitter started to just unwind as he fell into heavy sobbing. I reached over and just held this man as he cried so deeply. Ordinarily, I don't stop a reading to be the caretaker of the sitter; however, this man was so upset, that I found it to be perfectly natural for me to hold him at that moment.

As he calmed down I went back to work and basically recited what this young communicator said. This was one of those times where I was receiving my information through clairaudience which is not my usual way of working, but I always allow spirit to use whatever way they would like. I stay out of the way of deciding which way will be the best for that particular spirit, how could I possibly know anyways? I trust spirit one hundred percent and they have not steered me wrong yet. I try to be a dutiful employee for the spirit beloveds.

After the reading concluded I sat and had a conversation with this gentleman for about twenty minutes. I knew I had other sitters waiting but this was a special moment in this man's life and I wanted to see it through and be of help to him. He shared the story of Charlie and I am a better medium today because of this.

This Doctor was a gay male who came of age in a generation of gay men who lived their lives mostly in the closet or in secret. He was fortunate to have had a very long term relationship and had sadly lost his partner of more than thirty years about five years earlier to Altztheimers disease. He said most people knew that he was gay and he was sure that he lost some patients over the years when they found out about his sexuality. All in all, he said he was very much accepted and loved by his patients and he had a very successful practice. He was respected by fellow doctors because he was very good at his specialty and they referred patients to him just as he would refer patients to them.

He had known Charlie for a very short time and actually never met Charlie's parents. He liked Charlie and found him to be a very bright young man who was articulate in conversation about his future and his plans for college. After completing Charlie's physical and filling out the paperwork needed for his admission to the state university, he sensed some uneasiness in Charlie's demeanor. He knew instinctually that Charlie was also a gay man, what people today refer to as "gaydar." He felt that Charlie wanted to speak to him, but chose instead to quickly walk out of the exam room, thanking the doctor as he left. It bothered the doctor as in some ways, Charlie reminded him of himself at that age; questioning and not knowing exactly how to live the life of his true self. It nagged at this doctor that perhaps he could've questioned his patient to find out what was bothering him. After two weeks of second guessing himself, and just not feeling right about how Charlie left that day, he decided to call Charlie's home. When he called and announced himself as Charlie's doctor, the person on the other end of the phone call was Charlie's father. The doctor asked to speak to Charlie and there was a pause on the other end and then Charlie's father said, "I'm sorry, I guess you didn't hear, but Charlie died about two weeks ago; the little faggot told us he was a queer and then hung himself in our garage." The father's voice was quivering as he said to the doctor, "I'm sorry, I don't want to talk about this now, I'm not ready to" and he hung up the phone.

The doctor chose not to call back as he thought he would be causing more pain. The doctor was crushed and felt a responsibility for what had happened to his young patient. I felt this doctor's pain as he was telling the story that had been a part of his life for more than twenty years. Doc, as his patients called him, continued on saying that he was so angry at himself for not reaching out to that young man all those years ago and that the young man didn't have to die. "If only I had not been afraid of what people would say I would have been more assertive and had that conversation with Charlie and he'd still be here today." He was crying again and I took his hand and smiled at him and reminded him of what Charlie said as soon as he came through, "Stop blaming yourself, there was nothing you could have done." I asked the doctor, how could you know what Charlie was thinking at that point? Or that his family was so non supportive of their Charlie? You are not to blame yourself and you are not to carry this burden any longer. Charlie was a loving spirit who came all this way to relieve the anguish and hurt that this doctor had been feeling inside for many years. What a beautiful gift Charlie gave the good doctor that day. I was so proud of being even a small part of that healing.

A footnote to this story about the doctor and his patient Charlie is that, as the doctor explained to me, after our reading he came out of the closet completely and was active in a gay and lesbian organization that provides counseling for people who are struggling with their sexuality. Here was a man now in his seventies who understood the life lesson that he had learned. And he chose to use that lesson to do something so that there might be one less story like Charlie's. It was an honor for me to know this everyday angel walking the Earth doing what he could to make this world a better place. The last thing this wonderful human being said to me was, "Closets are for clothes, not people."

I know that many mediums work very hard at helping as many people as they can and sometimes don't have the luxury to stop and have a conversation after a reading because there are other clients waiting. I hope that my practice builds to the point where I am that well booked, but I promise you that I will always make the time for someone, even if it means losing the ability to stay on time with my appointments.

I recently did a transformative and healing reading for a television actor. His mother came through. I could tell that this lady had been a difficult person when she was still in the living. Her apologies and regrets were so sincere and deep that I just knew that she had been a tough cookie who may not have been the nicest mom to grow up with. I expressed her regrets and apologies. I was also shown that she had a serious issue with drinking. She was not your typical fun drunk, but rather a nasty foul mouthed abusive kind of drunk. He was very emotional during this reading and I kept going even though I sensed he needed to be comforted, however I chose to stay with my connection to spirit and let her have her chance to set things right, or at least try to. She showed me in a visual that she was bedridden at the end of her life and that her son was around and was in charge of her care, especially her end of life care. I also understood that there was another son and she seemed to have favored that son while they were growing up. My sitter was gay and his mother, more so than his father, had struggled with his sexuality. She shared, in this reading, the gratitude that she had for her actor son, as he not only chose to care for her after she had made his formative years a living hell, but also helped her maintain her dignity in her declining days. He sobbed throughout the reading and when it was over I sat and had a conversation with him. I find it hard to open up a person's deepest wounds and not feel the need to try and help pull them together at least enough to go back and have time to process all that they have been given from their loved ones in the spirit side of life.

The sitter shared with me how, while growing up and again when living back at home while struggling to get his acting career established, he was subjected to his mother's rants and taunts about him. She called him every name you can imagine and then some. She would humiliate him in front of her friends by referring to him as, "My little pansy," or "Nancy boy," and other times as "The little faggot that eats my food." I could not imagine the hurtful environment that this man grew up in. If the phone rang, she would yell to him "You better get it, it might be one of the other queers wanting to take you to the Ballet." I asked him how he tolerated it. He said it was horrible and it was something he would not wish on his worst enemy, but he was broke and had nowhere else to live.

Money had never been an issue for this man's parents who were people of some means, having been left a thriving business from his maternal grandfather. After his father had passed to spirit ten years earlier, his mother sold the everyday running of the business to a larger firm that had always wanted to acquire them. He said she did quite well as it was during the time when mergers and acquisitions were the way business was being done. She retained enough stock that she and a couple of generations to follow would be taken care of quite nicely. He made sure, after her diagnosis of liver disease that she had around the clock care. It was a struggle to keep finding new nurses as she was nasty and belligerent to them. She would not allow any African Americans to care for her, and he was embarrassed by the way she acted when he hired a wonderful nurse who happened to have been from Jamaica. He told me he paid the woman one month's salary just out of guilt for the humiliation she must have felt being in this home even though she hadn't even stayed until lunchtime.

The tears that this man shed that day were the greatest tears of his lifetime. They came from a place of healing and not from a place of hurt like so many tears before. I asked him what ever happened to the golden child, his brother. He said his brother pretty much squandered his life away and all of his money. He had become a drug abuser and an alcoholic who spent much of his adult life either in jail or in rehab. His brother had not really ever connected to life. He also said that he had no idea where his brother was anymore and that it made him sad that his brother chose to walk away from the family.

An interesting aside to this man's story is that after his mother's passing he learned from the family attorney that she had changed her will and basically disowned the drug-abusing son. The only money the brother had as his legacy was money and stock that had been left to him ten years earlier when their father died. My sitter went on to say that, much to his surprise, his mother had left almost everything to him and a sizable amount of stock to this man's life partner who he had been with for the last fifteen years.

It has been nearly two years since I did that reading and I recently heard from this man again. We met at a restaurant that his company owned, it was also part of his inheritance, and we had a nice conversation and a good meal. He updated me on his life, and shared that he was struggling at this point. One of his worst fears was now coming true. His life partner has become a heavy drinker and was starting to become verbally abusive towards him. He was considering ending the relationship because he could not go through his later years in a house of madness like he did his earlier years. I didn't give him any advice but I was a good listener and he kind of sorted things out that day. Since he had been in and out of counseling most of his life, he was very familiar with a particular counselor and he decided to not make any major decisions until he worked it out with this psychologist. He said he really respected her. I agreed that he had a good plan and he should trust that things have a way of working themselves out. He complimented me again about how meaningful the reading we shared was for him and how it helped him to start to heal. I reminded him that my part was the smallest part of the equation and this was between him and his mom. I hope he learned the lesson that his mother gave to him that day in her reading. I hope his life is fuller and kinder for the rest of his life. Love, acceptance and tolerance, are big lessons for us all.

17 "SMALL MEDIUM AT LARGE"
-ANONYMOUS

I have heard mediums in discussion groups complain about some of the newer methods of mediumship. Some take the stance that mediumship today is not as good as it was years ago. For me, it is a non-argument. Mediumship is not supposed to be like what it used to be. That would be like saying that science should stay the way it was a hundred years ago. All must evolve, mediums included! Yes it is true that people don't have the freedom to sit in development circles for years and years anymore like they used to. Yet, there are also advantages to being a medium in today's world. For one, people in general are just smarter and more educated than those a hundred years ago were which gives spirit much more to work with. My particular mediumship, shows me the benefits of so many cultural references that can spark visual stimulations which are available to today's mediums. These provide so much more to draw on, thus improving the level of evidence we can provide over what mediums had to work with in years gone by.

Many components make up a person's mediumship. How much development you have attained, the way you live your life, the environment of where you live, and mostly, how hard you have actually worked at your mediumship. It seems to me that far too many mediums get lazy and just settle into a style or technique that works for them. Think of your gift of mediumship as a plant. You cannot go against what is natural; you cannot make that plant grow any faster than it is supposed to. Nor can you neglect the plant and expect it to thrive and become a magnificent natural expression of the divine. The end product of your mediumship is the manifestation of so many parts and commitments to reach its most serviceable potential. Just as you cannot bribe nature to grow its plants any faster or any better, nor can you do that with your mediumship. It is an unfoldment and that requires time and hard work.

It is all about the quality of your mediumship and about how spirit will best be able to make use of your services. It is not about your notoriety or how many butts you can put in the seats of an event. Please keep in mind, that I do believe there is value in all mediumship, even in the lower levels of abilities. You may still be the right reader for that specific sitter that day and you may be of great help to them. If, however, you would like to help more people then I think it is in everyone's best interest that you strive to become the medium that spirit chose you to be, one who is meant to show by proof, that all survive their physical death, and that the love bonds between all people live on eternally.

"How do I prove it?" ought to be the question that you have in your mind now. To prove the continuity of life after death and that love survives all that nature can bring before it, you must be willing to become a real, credible medium, a medium that will make those in the spirit world proud to work with you. I promise you this spirit wants you to succeed and to be a great and healing medium, to help spirit do its work here on the physical plane. I know of no nobler cause than to be in service to those in the spirit side of life.

If it sounds to you like I am trying to give you a pep talk in order to encourage you to become the best medium you can, then you would be correct. I am a big fan of credible mediums and would love for there to be an increase in their numbers in my lifetime. I have committed to doing my work and I consider myself to be an employee for the best bosses in all the worlds: spirit. The rewards in becoming a credible working medium are immeasurable. How can you quantify being a part of an amazing event that can be transformative for so many hurting people who are reaching out for help? If one chooses to become a credible working medium that comes from a place of integrity in their mediumship, spirit will create the opportunities for you to help as many people as they need you to help. It is an interactive relationship between two worlds, here in the physical world and here in the spirit world. Did you notice I didn't say "there" in the spirit world? We must come to understand that "there" is closer to us than we tend to believe.

Is there a heaven and is there a hell? I get asked that question in almost every conversation I have with someone when we first speak. There is no hell. Even the Catholic Church, under the guidance of the new Pope Francis, has come out and said that it was never meant to be taken as a literal place. There is no hell. I have never seen anything in any reading to make me even entertain the possibility of its existing. Heaven is a more complicated question. My personal belief is that we all are spirits that have existed for eternity both past and future. We are part of a larger whole, which we may call God, or The One, The Source, whatever name one is comfortable with. I believe that when our time here on the physical side of life is over, we go back to our home on the spirit side of life. I believe that we may each experience a different initial version of what we go back to depending on what we need to see to help us in that transition. I think we all eventually return to the same "heaven." It may not look like clouds and angels and harps because that is not one of the visions that have been shown to me. I believe it to be more like the visuals I shared with you earlier. If you are a very religious person here, you may see Jesus or Buddha or whomever you feel connected to, but that is just for your transition and to help you return more gently with love.

We are responsible for our own version of our heaven. I think that many religions have shown us their versions of what they believe a heaven to be like. Because they have been organized and recognized by so many people, over an extended period of time, some organized religions' versions have become, for many, the accepted version of heaven. I don't agree that their version is the correct version of what heaven may be. I think it is such an individual process and solely reliant on our true belief based in our higher self. Put simply, you are responsible and in charge of what heaven is, for you. I am responsible and in charge of what heaven is for me. That is what personal responsibility is about, and how we perceive heaven to be is a personal communion between our physical life and our inner life. Part of what has transpired through the ages of man is that we have abdicated this responsibility to think for ourselves and just accepted an organized religion's version of what our heaven should be. We have become lemmings in this thought process and it is alright, there is no judgment attached to it except from my unique perspective as a medium, they are probably incorrect.

Why religions do things like this can be debated by better minds than myself. I am not really interested in changing anyone's relationship with their church or religion. I am, however, interested in offering my observation that, as a medium, what I have seen during many readings, while connected to the spirit world, differs from what I have learned about in other religions. I ask that you be open minded to the possibility that we as individuals have say in how we live, free will, and say in what happens to us after we stop living a physical existence. As a Spiritualist, I believe in personal responsibility. It is neither right nor wrong to think this way. It is a choice we have made to live our lives leading our lives as opposed to following some other doctrine as our pathway in this physical world. Spiritualists and many Spiritualist Churches that I have come to know accept people from all religions and tolerate all people.

My idea of what heaven will be like for me initially is it will be where I see all of the people that I have shared love with when I was on the physical plane. I believe it will be a place similar to where we are now, yet still somewhat different. I feel that it will be a more loving and peaceful existence based in a state of love that I think of as a state of grace. I think there will be beauty beyond the wonders of this beautiful nature that we experience here in the physical world. I see the coloring of my heaven to be more vivid and with more dimensional capabilities than that which we can comprehend with the brains that we have now. I believe that there will be animals just as there are here now, but I believe they will be treated with a different sense of respect and care than what we express in this life now.

Since my core belief as a human being is that we are spirits having a human experience, as opposed to humans having a spiritual experience, I believe we are ever-evolving and in a constant state of learning and moving forward to our God, Source, One or whatever name a person would need to connect to that which is a part of us and we are all a part of. I don't believe that our existence is random and without a higher purpose. I wrestle with the idea that there may be levels or various planes on the spirit side of life. I understand that was how pioneers of the Spiritualist movement have described it, but my gut tells me that they may have perceived it incorrectly based on what was accepted knowledge at the time they were alive, just as how I perceive it now may not be relevant or correct two hundred years from now. All things change and movement is progression so it makes no sense to think that even the spirit world is stationary and unmoving. All people evolve just as all times evolve. This is part of the human struggle; the constant, albeit slow, change that happens with or without our consent.

If we understand that the moon affects our ocean tides and our planet is constantly spinning, why would we think that what is in the spirit side of life would stay in one place? If we can at least accept that change is inevitable, then maybe we can get to a place where change is not as scary as it seems to be to most people. Again, free will; we could actually see change as a positive to be welcomed and encouraged, and not as something fearful to be avoided. If we are of the thought that heaven does exist then why should we limit what it is by the limitations of what our brains can come up with at this point. I truly believe that it does exist, but far differently than the most creative of us could imagine.

I have heard it said plenty of times that life on Earth is really hell. I don't buy into that idea. For one, I don't even think that hell is even a possibility. Two, I understand that this life can be unbearably difficult for many of our fellow human beings, but if this was truly hell, wouldn't it be that difficult for all human beings? Should I then believe that there are levels of hell? For me, after a while, it all unravels and just becomes too illogical to latch onto this premise. So my simple answer is, yes, there is heaven; one that is different than what many of us believe it to be now, but it does exist. And no, there is no hell. It never existed and probably never will as we are love-based spirits and I don't think we will evolve to being less love-based. Purgatory is something made up by leaders in churches that were more concerned about growing their power and used fear tactics to keep people under their control through fear. If you need some proof of this, study The Inquisition and the other atrocities of history that came from organized religions. I have never, not once in anyone's reading, seen anything suggesting that religion exists in the spirit world. It is a man-made idea that stays here in the physical world.

I have had the great fortune to have spent time with some of the great healers alive today. Some are known internationally and others work quietly behind the scenes in their own communities. These individuals have performed what most people think of as miracles. The healers themselves have no real abilities to heal any one, they act as a conduit for healing to come through for the person they are focusing on. In the Spiritist religion, healing is considered a more valued commodity than in almost all other religions that I am aware of. The most notable of Spirtist healers is Joao de Teixeira, also known as John of God. For more than forty years, John of God has been seeing thousands of people, almost daily, at his clinic in Abandania, Brazil. He travels to other countries as well to provide healing, however, many who have spent time at The Casa, as the clinic is known, say that it is a much deeper spiritual experience there and that the energy is otherworldly. I had the pleasure to have sat in the energy of John of God twice at The Omega Center in Rhinebeck, New York.

I went to see John of God the first time to pray for one of my brothers who was declining and near the end of his life after an extremely long-term illness. There were twelve hundred people there that day, many hoping for a miracle or possibly some relief from the illnesses they suffered with. There were many people there in wheelchairs and others who needed to be carried. As I sat in the morning session meditating, I realized that I would do my best in prayer for my brother and that I myself was in no need compared to those whom I sat with in the very large tent that was being used as a staging area for various groups and as a place for group meditations. It is a beautiful sight as everyone is asked to come dressed only in white clothing. My understanding is that it helps the "entities" that work with John of God to examine you.

As your group is called to leave the tent and go into the room where Joao sits you can feel the level of hope rise up. When you first come into the room where he is, the energy feels so different; for me it felt like I was walking through Jell-O. You are ushered up to him and he takes your hand for a few seconds and says something in Portuguese to his interpreter and you are then instructed what will happen for you next. I was told that I would get a spiritual intervention later that afternoon at two o'clock. At two o'clock I was back in the current as they call it; the energy of being in the same room as John of God. He pointed at me and had me sit in a chair just a few feet away from him. I thought that a bit strange but came to understand why at another time. In the room where the healer sat there were also about twenty mediums sitting in meditation, essentially acting as batteries for John of God. That may explain why I felt such an odd change in the energies in that room.

We were told that we should close our eyes and keep them closed, and to just stay quiet. It would take anywhere from about twenty to forty-five minutes. I heard Joao get up and walk around the front of the room where I was sitting and he said a few things in Portuguese to his interpreter. While in the current for that period of time I felt my eyes doing something very strange. They felt like they were darting around inside my head behind my closed eyelids, similar to what happens when we are in the REM stage of sleep. It felt as if it had lasted for five minutes. I later found out that we were in that state for nearly forty-five minutes. We were told to slowly open our eyes and quietly leave the room and go find a place to sit or lie down and to rest for an hour or so. They had provided many pads to lie on in grassy areas and it was a beautiful late summer's day so I did lie down and I rested.

I thought that day was an amazing experience and I followed their aftercare instructions that are meant to be followed for forty days. One of their instructions is to try to stay in bed between the hours of midnight and five am. They claim that is when the entities are working on us. The weirdest thing happened about two weeks after my spiritual intervention. Every night for the next three weeks I had the strangest occurrences while I was sleeping. I felt as if I was wide awake but at the same time I knew I was sleeping very deeply. I can't explain it any better than that. I had flashbacks to so many childhood memories. Most of these were memories that were either traumatic to me or very special to me. It seemed almost as if someone was exchanging the bad memories for better ones. Even though I had asked for others to be helped ahead of me, there was a request in my heart that some of the anxiety and occasional depression I would feel would be lifted and become more tolerable.

I can't really explain it well enough, but ever since that experience with John of God my anxiety has become almost nonexistent, and since then, I have yet to have a bout of depression. It's like someone came along and rewired my brain so that the things that used to trigger those events were no longer able to do so. I never had any really big problems with depression, but rather an occasional situational depression, usually brought on by the loss of a relationship or financial pressures. It's been almost five years since I had that healing and it has truly changed my life. I am grounded and my mediumship unfoldment escalated soon after that at a rate I had not experienced before. Interestingly, they announce each day which of the three entities that work with Joao is there, and for that day it was St. Ignatius of Loyola. My father's name was also Ignatius. Some might say that is just a coincidence; maybe so but I'd like to believe that my dad was also with me while I was in a sacred space within my soul. John of God has never charged anyone for a healing. Omega did charge a fee for the day. I am becoming less surprised how much spirit provides when you are doing God's work.

What I found out later from one of my teachers was that the reason John of God moved me and had me sit closer to him was that he was using me as part of his battery. I guess he sensed my connection to spirit and I was able to be of use for the healings that day.

If you are interested in learning more about some of the great healers of the past, you most likely do not have to go further than your own religion if you have one. Many of the great healers are the basis for the religions that came after they went to spirit. For me, the greatest healer would have to be Jesus of Nazareth. During his lifetime and most especially in the three years leading up to his crucifixion, he performed many healings which were deemed miracles by his followers then and are considered miracles still today. I believe that the best healers have also been some of the best teachers that humankind has been blessed with. Jesus was one of the most quoted and written about teachers and healers of all time.

In my reading and understanding of the history of Jesus and early Christianity, most of the texts were written anywhere from forty years after his death up to two hundred A.D. If you ever played the game of telephone where one person starts a message and whispers it to the next person and so on around a circle, then you know that by the time the message makes its way around the circle, it has usually changed significantly. I think that is what may have happened with the teachings of Jesus. If you want to read what is thought by many to be the most accurate account of the words that actually came out of the mouth of Jesus himself, read "The Lost Gospel Q." It is thought to have been written approximately fifteen years after his death. Its content is very similar to the parables and sayings that Jesus is most known for, but it is in a much less flowery or wordy writing. I think I understand what happened in the early days of Christianity. And I attest that I am by no means a student of theology or an expert on early Christianity. I am just sharing an opinion based on my readings and my understanding.

Jesus was a great teacher and healer and never traveled all that far from where he was born. Word of his accomplishments traveled much further, especially through the letters of St. Paul and also through the other early gospel writers. I think that his fame and popularity grew due to the need of the people at that time. The way that he was killed left him the ultimate martyr to fill that need. There was an orator named Stephen who was quite the crowd pleaser about forty years after Christ was killed. He drew much larger crowds and spoke about the same things as Jesus. He was also murdered and became a martyr but never reached the popularity of Jesus. History has a way of idolizing and demonizing, and time seems to be the buffer that polishes the stone that becomes the foundation for what we have come to accept as our heritage. Do I believe that Jesus is the son of God? Yes I do believe that, I also believe that he is not the only son of God, but rather we are all children of the same God.

I speak of Jesus and Christianity as I was raised Roman Catholic and this is a religion I have a small amount of knowledge about. I cannot speak to other major religions as I do not have a knowledge base. I don't believe that any one religion is more important or more right than any of the others. I think we are all connected with each other and all connected to the same God. I have my opinions and beliefs based on what are right for me as an individual. Just as fundamentalists in all religions would likely disagree with my beliefs, they choose to believe that which feels right to them. No one is right or wrong we are just allowed, with religious freedom in the United States, to choose that which fits us in the best way. I respect ALL religions and value their teachings and their leaders.

I am a Spiritualist and happy that I have found a religion that is based in inclusion and founded on the principles of love and respect for all. I believe you will find the tenants of this religion to be very similar to many other religions, perhaps with one major exception- we believe in personal responsibility for our transgressions. I also find it very interesting that the religion of Spiritualism is comprised mostly of former Roman Catholics and followers of other Christian-based religions. There are also a large number of people who choose Spiritualism as a religion, and Jewish as a culture.

I have also noted, in my unscientific observations, that many followers of Eastern religions such as Hinduism and Buddhism are also attracted to Spiritualism. From a limited vantage point, I have noticed too, that here in the United States, more times than not, people connected with Spiritualism come from a blue collar background. This may go back to this religion being started predominantly by women who, at that time in the United States, were not usually educated and who came from rural areas, steeped in poverty at the beginning of the Industrial Age.

This background of Spiritualism is another reason why a place like Lily Dale is so important to American history. It was what was happening on a larger scale across the entire United States at that time in history. Lily Dale was founded by free thinkers and it was one of the few places available for women to express their opinions at that time without suffering the repercussions had they done so in the general public arenas of the day. That may be why Susan B. Anthony and others in the suffragette movement chose to speak at Lily Dale in the early days of the Women's Movement.

18 NOT EVERY QUESTION IS MEANT TO BE ANSWERED

Sadly, there are questions which I, as a medium, am asked all too often and which I cannot answer. If God is a loving God, then why is there so much pain and suffering in this world? Or why did God take my child if he loves me? They are similar inquiries. The true answer to these types of questions is I don't know. I cannot presume to speak for God, but I can offer some ideas as to why life may seem to be as difficult as it sometimes is.

From everything I believe as a medium and as a spiritual person, I know that The Source, The One, The Almighty, God or whatever name you are most comfortable with, is a loving caring God. This is where Christianity has hidden behind the quote, "God works in mysterious ways." That line is not going to provide too much comfort to parents who have just lost their child on a cancer ward. The simple truth is people die. We are all going to die. We have an internal agenda of how and when that should happen, in a certain comfortable order, coupled with an unrealistic sense of fairness that doesn't actually exist.

Human beings are spirit first, with a soul that comes into a physical body predestined for a period of time that purportedly we agree to before we are even conceived. Life has never been fair anywhere during the history of humankind on this Earth, but we still insist on fairness being given to us. That is not a realistic approach to human existence. Perhaps the sense of fairness we assume we are entitled to, is actually something to strive for as we evolve as a species. But it doesn't exist in humanity in a consistent, dependable manner at this time. Anytime we lose a loved one who is younger, we think it was too soon, but honestly who are we to decide that timeline? For all we know maybe the soul that entered that body at conception was already more evolved and chose to be in a physical body that would not be here for a very long time in this physical world. We are limited in our thinking by the limitations of what our brains can comprehend.

We have an understanding of time as being linear. Suppose that time doesn't exist in the spirit world the way it does here. I have been shown by spirit in readings that time is merely a human experience that stays with us here on this planet. What has been shown to me is that, if you are twenty years old and your mother dies, yet you live another sixty years, your experience of that passing will be that it will be sixty years until you are reunited with your mother. However, your mother's experience of the same scenario is that you are but a moment away from her at any point in time. For you, sixty years must pass, for her, a second later, and she is reunited with her loving son. Now the question is what loving God takes a mother from her son? Or is that a loving God who creates a place where a mother will be reunited with her son in only a moment after her physical death? They are one and the same loving God. We are egotistical to believe that our way of thinking is the only way to perceive things. This is what I mean by the limitations of our brains. We have not yet evolved to the place where time and space are no longer relevant to us. But I think that is where we are headed as human beings.

Many times during a reading I see a small spirit with another grown up spirit. I have come to understand that this small spirit is a spirit that did not make it through the birth process; it is an aborted or miscarried spirit. Human beings are often judgmental. Some people won't even like that I have put those two examples together with miscarriage generally afforded a more honorable acceptance than abortion. The truth is, there is no judgment in the spirit world. They live in a state of eternal love; a state of grace. All spirits are equal and all spirits are loved and none of that love is based on Earthly human prejudices. A spirit is a spirit is a spirit. Even if the spirit only lived for a minute in our time, it is valued and loved as if it lived to be a hundred years old in Earth time. If the word spirit is becoming difficult for you to think of in those terms then just switch the word for baby. Is a baby any less valuable to their parent if it happens to die too early and not according to our scale of importance? Of course not, so why would we place a lesser value on spirit? Because we are not as evolved as we think ourselves to be. We will get there one day, to a more loving caring understanding of the value of each and every spirit. When we do that is when we will truly understand just how loving our God is.

When we get to the place where all humans treat each other with the acceptance and love that our God has for us, then humankind will have reached the point where wars between different factions will no longer be relevant and other, better choices will be made using the gift that our loving God has given us, free will. This time in this life is tough for some and extremely tough for others. I have heard it called Earth School. This is the place where spirits go to learn certain valuable lessons that are sometimes very hard to learn. That is why some people perceive this life as a living hell; it can be that difficult for some people. Here is where gratitude and compassion for all other people becomes most important and very necessary. The mystics of the past have spoken of this importance.

The most difficult limitations that we confront in our lives are the ones that we put there. They are the limitations of our thoughts and beliefs. If we believe we cannot do something, we most likely will not be able to do that thing. If we change our perceptions, we could probably overcome many limitations. To do so, we must be open to changes. Change is inevitable and should be desired when it can be, for change holds the treasures of our potentials beyond our preconceived notions of our self and our believed capabilities. If you walk around looking towards the ground all day long you may not see the rest of the world that is happening at eye level and above. Awareness is a component of change. If you are in the process of raising your awareness, you are on the path of changing. You don't actually know who you are except at any given moment. You are not who you were and you are not who you will be, you only truly can know yourself in this time that is now. That is why you have heard it said so many times and in differing ways, be present in your own life. We only exist in the now.

The past is gone and only exists as a memory, the future has yet to happen so it is not real yet; but this moment of your life, right at this exact moment, is the most important moment in your life because it is real, and it counts and you matter in that moment. As mediums, we learn to still our thinking minds just enough to be able to raise our awareness of other opportunities for communication that are available right at that exact time. If the medium is thinking about yesterday's events or about lists of things to do during the day, they are not available to those in the spirit world to communicate with. They can only connect to us in the present tense; not in the past tense or in the future tense. This is another reason why many mediums practice quiet meditation; they understand that it is the art of being present in your own life. It is essential for each of us to learn our own ability to work with the divine inside each of us.

Many of the better mediums spend years working out their personal issues before they ever attempt to help sitters through whatever life situation has brought them to the reading. As a medium, if you are so full of angst or anxiety in your own life, you may be of limited value to your sitters. It is in everyone's best interest that you face your issues and do your best to work through them. If you don't tackle the things that have held you hostage in your life, you will most likely bring your own issues into your sitter's reading and that would be less than helpful for the person who has trusted you to help them through your connection to the spirit world. All people will have stress and problems. Mediums are human beings and they are likely to have their own set of issues. The better effective mediums are the ones who were willing to put in the time and hard work to conquer theirs.

Just as a medium should have realistic expectations of what their abilities are, so should the sitter have realistic expectations of what the medium can do to help them at the time of need in their life? As a medium, what we can do is we can help you through your grieving process by communicating with loved ones on the spirit side of life. We can bring through adequate evidence so that you know there is life after the transition from physical to spiritual. We can offer you ways to cope with whatever the situation is that you are dealing with.

What your medium cannot do: we cannot bring your loved one back to this physical world once they have died a physical death; we cannot make up for all the wrongs that life has dealt you; we cannot lift curses or spells because they do not actually exist and never have; we cannot give you the winning lottery numbers, if we could don't you think we would have won already? So please stop asking for that, I hear that at least twice a week, every week; we cannot solve all of your problems, for the most part mediums are rarely psychotherapists but we can share some pretty good insight into some areas of your life that may be beneficial to you.

Most credible mediums have made a life choice to live a life of service to fellow human beings while serving those in the spirit world and it is an honorable choice. Please be respectful of the medium as s/he is truly a sensitive being. That is how mediums are able to do what it is that they do. They are just more sensitive than most people, some more than others. I have heard it said that the price of sensitivity is sensitivity! The old time mediums in Europe were of the mindset that a medium was very similar to a fine musical instrument. The better care you gave to the instrument, the better sounding the music that could be played on it. If a medium understands their gift and treats it with the care and respect that is needed for it to be finely tuned, then they are the mediums that will achieve greater capacity for serving spirit on a much higher level and they will be the mediums that you hope to find.

A medium is a student for life. They are constantly learning more and more about their own spirituality and that leads to enhancement of their natural gifts of mediumship. If you find that a medium has become unwilling to study and put in the time of introspection that is needed for their own growth, you will most likely find a medium that is repetitive and not truly serving spirit at their highest level. Some mediums believe that their gift may lessen with the aging process, but the truth is age is irrelevant to mediumship. More than likely those mediums no longer work as hard at their development. A medium must continue to develop their abilities all through their lives. Remember, a student for life!

19 HOW TO GET THE BEST READING YOU CAN FROM A MEDIUM

As a working medium I think I can offer some tips that can help you get the best one to one reading possible from your medium. Before I do any reading, I ask that the reading I am about to do be healing and meaningful, and come from a place of love for the highest good of all involved. Some mediums say a prayer before each reading; others just have a quiet moment for themselves to put themselves into the right head space. No two mediums are alike, so try not to pay too much attention to their individual techniques. More than likely, if your medium is one who works from a place of integrity, they have already done the self-preparation that they use in their mediumship. If your medium seems to be one who works from volume, don't be put off by that. I've seen some amazing readings done in a very short amount of time with very high levels of mediumship at work. Most mediums would not be able to sustain their energy or their link with the spirit world for too long working in that manner. There are exceptions. Allow the medium the privilege to work the way they feel is their highest level.

I always ask my sitters to come to a reading with an open mind and an open heart. This is truly the pathway to communication for the blending of the three components of mediumship: the spirit discarnate, the sitter incarnate, and the medium that facilitates the communication. I also ask my sitters to ask their loved ones to come to me as I believe this is similar to an invitation to a meeting and your loved ones don't know me so it is just the polite thing to do and I believe those on the spirit side of life appreciate the respect that is shown. In the beginning of all readings, I ask my sitters to not say no to any information I bring through in the first few minutes of their reading as it can sometimes take a few minutes for the blending of the energies involved to hit the "zone." I find that by doing this, I don't have to spend energy rebuilding the energy from repeated "No"s. If I am incorrect, and I very well could be at that point, I ask that they give me a neutral response such as "I'll think about that" or "I'll remember you said that." Within a short period of time, and as long as we keep building the energy together, it always gets to the "zone." It has never not gotten there, unless, of course, the sitter is being difficult or is far too negative.

I have also found, after doing so many readings, that far too often the things that the sitter was inclined to say no to originally, they will realize what the connection was, and the nos become yesses. I can't even guess at how many emails I have received from sitters after their readings, reversing their original response from negative to positive confirmation of the information provided. I am speaking here from the perspective of one to one readings; however, the effect of too many negative responses during a public display of mediumship kills the energy there too and can make for a very long service for the medium and the other people in attendance. A poor receiver can actually ruin the evening's mediumship. The more highly trained mediums will usually spot this happening and will move off of that person quickly so as not to kill the energy for the rest of the service.

I think I have found a better method for some sitters so that they will receive the best reading possible from that particular medium at that exact time. If you have any doubts as to whether you will get a good enough reading, here's what I would suggest you try as the sitter. Be so enthusiastic that it automatically raises your vibration (energy). In turn, the medium will raise their vibration (energy) and I believe that your reading will just go a whole lot better and the medium will not have to spend your time trying to raise your energy for you in order to get a better reading. Those in the spirit side of life respond to higher positive energy. I promise you that those in spirit want to hear from you just as much if not more than you want to hear from them. Do everything you can to aid the process. It is for your benefit in your reading. Don't try to take over the reading, as that would be totally counterproductive, but do all that you can to show up for your sitting in a positive upbeat mood with hopes for the best possible connection to those in the spirit world.

Here is a mistake that some sitters make that can throw off a reading. Try not to haggle over the price of the reading. Most mediums have put in many years of training to get to the place they are at and they have set their fees according to what they believe is correct for them and their abilities. Most credible Spiritualist mediums are not so materialistic that they charge way beyond the true value of their service. Remember, mediums have mortgages and children and bills just like everyone else. I have even heard stories from mediums who have actually cancelled sitters' appointments when they became too aggressive about trying to get "a better deal." If the medium you have chosen is beyond your budget it would not be impolite to mention that in a nice way to the medium. If the medium is able to help you, they may choose to do that. If you are truly unable to pay, you can always find a medium to help you they have chosen to live a life of service. Be fair though, don't use the "I'm broke" story unless it is true, and otherwise think about the energy you are bringing to your own reading. I believe that every beautiful credible mediumship reading is a small miracle that we are all blessed to be participating in, so please value the reading with the respect that communicating with your loved ones deserves. There is a connection to the spark of divinity in each reading, a true blessing that has been created from a place of love and compassion.

20 "TRY A LITTLE TENDERNESS"
-OTIS REDDING

I wish I had a brick for every time I talked to someone about the value of forgiveness in their life. I'd probably have a beautiful four bedroom house by now! The act of forgiving someone for how they have wronged you is huge in the human experience. It is the single greatest gift a person can give to himself. It can also be one of the hardest, most incredibly difficult things to do; to let go of the hurt and anger that has embedded itself deep inside you, so deep that you sometimes feel it has become part of your core. The truth of the matter is, it is not nor could it ever become a part of your core. At our core level all humans are loving and compassionate by nature. We are born with an innate ability to nurture and care for each other. This is why we choose to connect with other human beings and form relationships. Then you might ask, how can we explain people like Hitler or Stalin or Charles Manson? They are aberrations of the human condition. Thankfully they are not the norm but an extreme of what can go wrong in a human life experience. They are psychotic in psychological terminology. If you go back through the history of mankind you will sadly find that people like this have always existed. We understand those who are like this to be the worst of the worst through our collective history.

Have they actually served a purpose with their perverted mindsets of heinous values? Greater minds than mine will have to figure that one out. I believe that all human beings, even those we come to despise because of their actions against humanity, have played a role in what we as a human race has decided what is good and evil. Families that have lost loved ones through the atrocities of these beings will struggle to forgive those who inflicted the deepest of human pains. As time moves forward and people become removed from the pain, generation after generation, there may come a day when forgiveness will happen. The events will never be forgotten, nor should they be, as history has a way of repeating itself if we choose not to learn from it. For individuals there may be little value in this level of forgiveness, but as a whole society may one day find value in allowing these tragic events to become healed for the good of all that come after us. It is not healthy for this type of hate and anger to live within our humanity; there is no positive value in this hatred hundreds of years later. The loved ones cannot be brought back. The sick criminals who perpetrated these events are long gone, yet we as a human race will still be carrying this hate inside us on a cellular level if we never forgive. These types of pain become part of our DNA and we have the free will to release ourselves from that pain by the act of forgiveness. In the release of this pain and much deserved anger, there are a freedom and a hope that maybe one day there will be no more of these demented people acting this way towards their fellow human beings.

I am truly sorry for any family that has suffered because of the loss of loved ones by the horrors of our histories. It has been nearly seventy five years since the time of Hitler and Stalin, yet the pain is still so real for many people walking this Earth. Since then there have been others like Idi Amin and Pol Pot and still others today oppressing and killing their own peoples. Sadly, this may be part of the human condition, but there can be hope that it will end within a few generations after we are gone from our physical life on this planet. Time may be a human creation to help us understand where we are and where we have been, but it also has the ability to numb us to the pains of yesterday. If you go back through the ages you will have found other horrific humans that were despicable in the things they did to others. Vlad the Impaler lined the roads with the heads that he beheaded to scare the next villages into surrendering before he even got there. The crosses that lined the roads during the reign of the Roman Empire were a constant reminder to the people that were being oppressed of just how little hope they had to escape the power hungry meanness that they lived under. The atrocities done by the Roman Catholic Church during The Inquisition were unbelievably horrific.

The point I hope to make by citing these other examples of human to human horrors is that time has played a role in alleviating the depths of pain for the loved ones of all victims. Simply put, there are no more directly related loved ones of those who suffered these events in history. When was the last time you heard someone say that they hated all Romans because their great great great great etc. grandfather was hung on a cross? When have you ever heard someone spew anger towards Vlad the Impaler for what he did to their family? This is the gift of time in human terms. We will never forget that these things happened, just as we will never forget the things that Hitler did, or Stalin, but time will allow for a collective opportunity to forgive the past one day, and maybe at that point, humans as a whole will have evolved to a place where this meanness will no longer be in our DNA and all people will live a kinder gentler existence. That crossroad would present one of the most important opportunities for our use of free will. We can choose to live a more loving and compassionate life here on Earth or we can carry forward the negativity that belongs to our past with us into our present lives. It is our responsibility and our obligation to decide if forgiveness is available to all human beings or just to the ones that we as a society decide are deserving of it. I believe all are worthy of forgiveness one day, maybe not this day, but one day, when history deems it correct.

Far too often in readings a loved one will come through and offer apologies for the ways they have wronged their loved ones here in the physical world and I always pass that information on to the recipient. I know that these messages are some of the most life-transforming moments a person can have. There have been times when the sitter refuses the apology and I know that the pain is still so real to that person that they may not be ready to be able to forgive yet. I do, however, try to help them to understand that this apology, though not accepted, is something they should remember, for the time may come one day when they will be ready to hear it and then they will decide that they forgive the discarnate who has wronged them. Once, while meditating, I felt a spirit come to me and he was trying to apologize to me and I recognized him immediately. I felt fear, an old fear. I knew I was safe as this person who scared me so terribly when I was just a boy had long been gone and could no longer hurt me. I allowed the apology to continue and it was heartfelt and sincere. He was apologizing for scaring me so much and asking for my forgiveness for the way he acted and especially for his actions on one particular day.

It was unusually warm for a late autumn day. I didn't realize that my long sleeved shirt would be too warm for hanging out at the ice house with my friends. We had a lot of places like the ice house in our neighborhood. Great adventures were always the plan but none as great as the one remembered for this day. As soon as you turned into the driveway of the ice house, the one thing you couldn't help but notice was the overwhelming smell of ammonia. As kids we often played on this site as long as we didn't get chased away by any of the workers. As an adult, I have thought of how dumb it was to be using this place as one of our playgrounds. Was the ammonia that permeated the air going to kill us later in life? Or could one of us have gotten hurt flying up and around the massive pipes that pumped the chemicals into the factory building? The truth is the only serious injury I can recollect was when one of the older girls broke her leg when she caught her ankle in a hole in the ground.

The other injury I remember was once when I lay down in the grass near the fence to the back of the property, I accidently put my elbow down on a queen bee. One of those large ones, the kind that aren't supposed to sting you, unless of course you accidently almost kill one with your body's weight. My arm swelled up huge, it was so cool. There was a creek that ran alongside of the ice house factory that fed into the Saw Mill River that ended into the Hudson River near the city pier down in Getty Square. The creek or as we called it "the crick," sat about twenty feet below the driveway and was held in place by walls, both manmade and natural stone. This was the same creek that took the life of my father's best friend when he was a little boy. They were swimming about a quarter of a mile from where I stood that day. They weren't supposed to be swimming there but, you know, boys will be boys. From the way my father told the story, his friend stepped on a rock in the water and it just caved in and the boy got swallowed up by what today would be called a sink hole. They never found the kid's body and it had a profound effect on my father and, I would assume, on the other half dozen or so kids that were swimming there that day. My father never wanted us to go near that creek, but that never stopped us; what could possibly happen down at the crick?

There was an empty abandoned truck box parked on the side of the driveway next to the wall of the creek. We had made it a clubhouse of sorts, by dragging a junky couch and some ratty chairs into it. For a while we would go there when someone could swipe some cigarettes or if we bought a "loosey" from the bookie who owned the candy store. Louie the bookie would always sell you a cigarette out of his own pack for two cents. You could get matches for free just about anywhere back then. There might be four kids sharing one butt or if you were lucky you might have had one all to yourself. I wasn't the youngest kid there but I was the smallest. Even though I had just turned eleven, I probably could've passed for eight or nine years old. Around the neighborhood the ladies who sat in front of the stores used to refer to me as the "lawyer" or "the mouth" since I was the one who usually had to talk to the cops or the grownups when things went wrong. I now confess that it wasn't any special ability to speak that gave me that role; I was just the slowest runner and couldn't get away as fast as the other kids. I guess trying to talk my way out of situations was a survival technique that came with the territory of being the one with the shortest and slowest legs.

This one day, one of the guys had brought a lock and a key with him and we were going to lock up the club so that we could control who went in. I remember thinking to myself, who gets to hold the key or could we all get keys? As we were standing there debating the key issue, three of us were inside the club and another five were standing on the ground near the open doors when someone yelled out "John! "Everybody reacted when we heard his name. John was one of too many drunks in our neighborhood. What made John different was that if he got close enough to you he would smack you or try to kick you, and he was a lot bigger than any of us. So everybody who could ran and scattered like roaches when someone turns on the lights. He was headed for the truck body and I was trying to get down as fast as I could. I remember looking up and seeing my brother taking a quick left out of the ice house driveway going towards Doyle Park. It didn't occur to me then that my own brother wouldn't stay to help me but instead fled to save his own butt. I had to climb down from the truck, I couldn't jump, and it was too high for me. John had never hit me but I didn't want him to have his chance that day.

Fortunately, one of the other kids, I don't remember who, was also in the truck and when he jumped he stumbled and John went after him. As I hit the pavement, John turned from the other kid and came towards me. John was a scary looking guy to a kid. He was obviously bigger than we were and almost always staggeringly drunk. Whenever you saw John on the streets and there were other adults around, he seemed almost nice. If you had wanted to tell someone that John was mean to the kids they probably wouldn't have believed you. After all, we were just stupid little street kids. Who was going to believe us over a polite grown up even though he was a drunk or a rummy as my father would say. The one thing that scared me the most about John was that he had this weird bump that went from behind his right ear down the side of his neck. I didn't know what it was but, man I never saw anybody that had anything like that before and I was scared of it and him. He came at me then and I tried to run to his left because the wall down to the creek was just to the right of him. He lunged at me and made a snarling sound like a strange kind of determined grunt. He grabbed my arm and I started to cry because I was so scared. I wriggled and moved as fast as I could to try and get away. I ended up on the ground and I couldn't get up. He pulled me up off of the ground like I was weightless. Before both of my feet even hit the ground again I had wriggled enough so that the only thing that John had any kind of grip on was the sleeve of my long sleeve shirt. He tried to get a better grip and spun around to try and control me. For a split second I could see that he had lost his balance and I pushed against him to get free from his grip. His footing started to give way as he tried to regain his balance, but he couldn't. He must have been too drunk and he bounded down the side of the wall towards the creek. I didn't see him fall as I was scrambling to get back on my feet and I started to run as fast as my little legs could go. I remember at the end of the ice house driveway I turned right and headed towards the Flying A gas station where my father's friend worked. As I crossed the little bridge that went over the creek below I looked over to see if John was coming after me. He wasn't. He was lying at the bottom of the rock wall right next to the water but not in the water.

Even though I only looked for a second, I somehow knew from the position of his body that John was not getting up right then to come after me. I ran to the gas station and I was breathing hard. When I got there the men were busy and didn't notice me. I stayed there for a few minutes and then walked home; the long way home. I didn't go back over the bridge past the ice house which was only a block and a half from my house, but instead I walked about six blocks in the opposite direction towards my home. I never saw John the drunk again. None of us kids ever saw John the drunk again. No one had seen what had happened and I never told anyone about that day until I was grown up. It has been more than forty five years since that day and I can still feel how scared I had been, and sometimes how guilty I felt. I resolved it in my mind as an act of self-defense.

As I recently connected with who I believed to be John the drunk who had tried to kill me, I saw a scene of him in a Veterans hospital and they were telling him that the cancer had spread and there was no hope or treatment. All through my life I had felt a certain degree of guilt relating to that story of the day in the ice house parking lot. Had I caused this man to die? Was I at all responsible? The sense from the apology that I felt from his spirit was one of sorrow for scaring me. I believed him to be a veteran of the armed services because of seeing him in a Veterans Hospital setting. I came away after that meditation visitation feeling that a tremendous gift had been given to me that day. I no longer felt any sense of guilt about his passing. He had been a horrible drunk who did inflict pain on children because of his own internal rage and it was not specifically aimed at me. I let go of the fear and guilt I had carried. Although I knew on a thinking level that I did not cause this man's death, I somehow had been victimized by the fear I felt that day. I have come to forgive John for the way he treated me and others. I understand on some level that he was a troubled soul who probably had a difficult life and tried to numb his way through life with alcohol. My forgiving John for treating me badly turns out to be a gift to me and I hope a gift to him as well in spirit. Was he truly a bad man? As a child I would have said yes, but now as an adult who understands the value of forgiveness I see John as a victim also and I feel compassion for the life he led.

I am of the mindset that we are all one people. I would have to forgive John, which of course is indirectly forgiving myself. It is the gift of the change of perception that was shared with me while connected to spirit for myself. I did not take his life and I was not responsible for his actions. I did my best to stay alive in a situation where I could've very easily been thrown down that wall by John in his fit of rage. I now see this man as someone who was dying already and was angry at someone, maybe everyone. Who knows? I know that he had been a soldier who served his country and by the age he was at that time, he probably served in World War Two. Maybe the scenes he saw or participated in were behind the anger and need to drink. I don't know, but I feel compassion for his soul and know that someday he and I will meet again and I will then know the answers to the how and why's of our paths crossing. I have come to understand the value of forgiveness because of this man that I so long held bad feelings towards. I no longer see him that way and I accepted his apologies. He meant them and they came from the right place in his heart. I wish him well and send him love.

21 WHERE SWEETNESS LIES

I have the utmost respect for the people who have honored me by allowing my participation in communication from this world to the next on their behalf and at their request. There is still another of the " clairs" that I have not spoken of; it is one that I have experienced but have not heard other mediums talk about it. There are times during a reading where the spirit communicator will want to show an enormous emotional response to the sitter. An example of this which I wrote about previously had to do with a child I saw in spirit who was shown to me to have passed to the spirit world, and was being taken care of and loved. The spirit loved ones who wanted to show me how loved this child was sent a wave of emotion through me that was not only incredible to feel, but felt pure and genuine in a way that I had not known love in this lifetime. It felt as if someone just poured a very warm thick liquid over my head and it flowed through me like melting honey. It was both sweet and warm. More importantly, I was able to describe the feeling to the sitter as what was being shown to me was truly meant for them. I was just the vessel for this exchange of deeply felt emotion. I looked to find a word that described this light filled wave of emotion in a reading, and I could not find one, so I have given it the name of clairamorance. Clair meaning clear, and amorance meaning pure love. I am always grateful when spirit chooses to share this special 'clair' with me for the loved one sitting across from me. It is a double sided pleasure. For all I know maybe other mediums experience this phenomenon as well and place it under the heading of clairsentience but for me it does not belong there, it is different.

I was recently reminded in a conversation with a friend of the beauty of true clairaudient communication. Noreen had a younger sister who was developmentally challenged and was quite childlike in her manners and demeanor despite her being middle aged at the time of her passing from a bout with cancer that took her to the spirit side of life. Bridget had the sweetest little voice, breathy and childlike. As I got out of my car one day, and before I started toward the front door of my friend's house, I heard Bridget's voice most clearly, and in her very distinctive tone she called my name, "Jake". I heard it repeatedly and looked in the direction from which it came but saw no visual of Bridget. It did put a smile on my face to hear her unique voice again after her passing to the spirit side of life. When I shared this clairaudient contact with Noreen it brought my friend to tears as she was having an extremely bad day and so needed to know that her younger sister was alright. Spirit or God does work in the most mysterious ways. My friend's mother, who was in her early eighties and had taken care of Bridget for all of her days, had also passed to spirit just four weeks before Bridget.

Bridget was in the Emergency Room of a local hospital and there was a severe ice storm and the hospital became so overrun with people getting hurt in accidents due to the ice, that Bridget was unable to be admitted to ICU and was instead sent to another floor. Her doctors decided to do a procedure to help with the difficulty of breathing that Bridget was experiencing. The doctors told Noreen that they were going to attempt to do this procedure without anesthesia as they did not have access to it in that part of the hospital. Noreen tried to stop them saying that she didn't think Bridget would allow it and it would probably agitate her; the doctors shushed Noreen and had her wait in the lounge area while they attempted the procedure. Bridget did become extremely agitated and they were not able to do the procedure. They asked Noreen to come back to help calm her sister down.

It was a very dark and cold January evening with an ice storm that nearly crippled the area. As she held Bridget's hand, Noreen spotted a beautiful lady bug crawling between her and Bridget. She pointed the lady bug out to Bridget who couldn't speak as she had a tube in her throat. Bridget's eyes brightened, however, and she immediately calmed down. Noreen was sure that like herself, Bridget had sensed her mother's strong presence around them. Noreen was just amazed at seeing a lady bug in the middle of winter during an ice storm settle in between the two sisters. Just days later, Bridget, with her devoted sister Noreen at her bedside, took her last breath and went home to the spirit side of life. After leaving the hospital and returning home Noreen grabbed the handrail on her front steps, she looked down at her hand and there was that ladybug just sitting there. She felt her mother's presence and began to cry. She knew that her mom had come to comfort her after welcoming Bridget back home.

About a year later in a reading that I did for Noreen I felt the sweet energy of Bridget, her message was for her sister to go ahead and get that ladybug tattoo. It's been done and is on Noreen's ankle. My sense is that this mom went ahead to make sure that someone would be there for Bridget as her time drew to an end here on the physical side of life. Even in death a mother's love is always there.

My friend Noreen knew of my abilities and was very helpful to me early in my development in many different ways. I have always done some handy man type of contracting work as a second job throughout much of my adult life and was working in her home one day when I felt her mother's presence. I sat and got myself to a quiet place. I had a notepad and a pen in my lap and within a few minutes her mother had given me so much information that it filled a few pages of the pad. When I was able to sit with Noreen and share what had come through from her mom of course she was happy and emotional but there was one most interesting part that I didn't understand at first. Her mother had mentioned to me that there was something of value hidden in her closet and to me it felt like money and she wanted to make sure that Noreen would find it. My friend had gone through the closet and indeed found money that her mother had stashed away.

Spirit does work in the most extraordinary ways. I came to my friend's house one day not long after and she handed me an envelope which had a gift certificate inside for a week course at The Arthur Findlay College for Psychical Studies in Stansted, England. Any medium who is truly interested in their own development longs to take classes at Stansted. My friend wanted to thank me for the gifts her mom and sister had shared through me and to show her appreciation she wanted to do something nice for me. This was the single most generous gift I had ever received in my life and to be honest, the most meaningful. I was able to go to England and I also added more study time on there as the airfare is so expensive that it just made sense to stay longer. Spirit found a way to get me to Arthur Findlay College and the love and generosity of this family made it all happen.

As a side note to this story, all mediums have signs or symbols or visuals that take us to pieces of information, almost at times acting as bridges to more information for our sitters. Bridget has chosen so generously in spirit to help me in my work by appearing in my mind's eye when I am to know that there is a special needs person connected to my sitter. Whenever I feel Bridget's energy I can't help but smile because she was so childlike in nature but now chooses to stay connected to me to help others. So here was a mother who selflessly made sure her daughter kept the money safe. Here is the selflessness of Noreen who then shares this money to afford me my first class at Stansted. And most important is the selfless act of Bridget who chooses in her after life to help me bring comfort to other families that happen to have someone with special needs in their family. So when I hear people talk about angels, my mind tends to turn towards the ones that I refer to as everyday angels walking this Earth. This particular family has their share of these everyday angels and I am blessed to have known them.

Clients have asked me about their loved ones who have passed from the physical life, wondering if they are still sick on the other side. I say "No." I have never seen a spirit that is still sick. Remember that they no longer have the limitations of a physical body so there is nothing there to get sick. They are pure spirit upon their arrival back home. Yes, back home. I believe when we pass from this life to the next we actually go home to where we came from. The loved ones here are sad and grieving but those in spirit are having a different experience of this passing. They are celebrating the return of someone they love and that this loved one is no longer struggling with the physical world's issues. It is a joyous time. I wish we could come to see all death this way, however, I know I'm being a bit idealistic.

We have to wonder about if a spirit makes a choice before coming into a body why would they ever choose to be in a body that is wracked with pain or limited by disease and so many difficult possibilities. I don't have a clear cut answer to this age old question, but I do believe that all beings are valuable, no one any more valuable than another. It may be that we need to see and care for others who have such an incredibly hard existence to teach us the importance of love and compassion or the tolerance and acceptance for all people, physically or mentally ill.

Spirit comes into the physical world at the point of conception and there is no judgment about how long that spirit is here on this physical plane. I believe an aborted spirit is just as loved and valued as a spirit that was able to stay on this Earth for one hundred years. All spirits are valued and loved as one and the same. We are all a part of something greater than ourselves as individuals and should learn to appreciate all elements of the human condition, including those who we perceive as different from ourselves. All spirits have the same spark of divinity residing in their beings, so who are we to say one is more valued or important than another? We have so much more evolving to go through, and the main ingredient that drives that evolvement is, and has always been, love.

After finishing my fifth reading in this beautiful home I knew I had one more reading to go before I could head home. The hostess approached me before my next sitter came in and asked me if there was any chance that I might be able to squeeze another sitter in at the end of the night. I asked her very politely if there was a true need for the reading or was this just someone who was curious about spirit? She relayed that this was a friend who had come by just to hear the other sitters talk about their readings with me, which is fairly common when you do this many readings in a row at someone's home, but she did think that Nancy could really use my help. I said, "Of course," and assured her I would do my best.

At that time of my development, I was limiting my readings to no more than six per evening. This would be my first time doing a seventh reading in a row but I felt strong and I was not the least bit tired. Interestingly, I don't usually get tired from doing the readings and working with spirit energy for that long a period of time. Instead, it usually has just the opposite effect on me; I get wired up and can sometimes struggle to sleep when I get home. After I finished my sixth scheduled sitter, I asked for a minute to just sit and be in the quiet just to ask spirit for help as I always do with each reading that I do. I asked that the reading be healing and meaningful, and come from a place of love, and be for the highest good of all involved.

It was already after midnight, however, I felt that this very sweet lady named Nancy needed to connect to spirit and that this might be the only chance she would ever have as we sat down I immediately felt the energy of a youngish male who told me that he had a broken heart and had died from a massive heart attack. In my mind's eye I saw the old television character Grizzly Adams and I described this visual to her. She understood who I was talking with. I said that he was a very large man with a full beard and his hair was pretty long, but that I sensed a gentle quality about him, and I described him as a gentle giant. With that Nancy started to cry. I explained to her that I believed he had had his heart broken when he was in his early twenties and I thought him to be in his late thirties at the time of his transition to the spirit side of life. She did not have any knowledge of him ever having his heart broken, but maybe it happened and she wasn't aware of it.

For some reason he showed me the upper West Side of Manhattan and then very quickly he showed me Grand Central Terminal in midtown Manhattan. I had an old girlfriend who lived on the Upper West Side so I knew the streets that he was imprinting to me. I had also been in Grand Central Terminal many times as I use the trains to take advantage of seeing plays and concerts in Manhattan as I only live about thirty five minutes north of Manhattan. Nancy continued to dab her eyes with a tissue as I continued. I understood from his energy that this was her older brother and he gave me the name of Dave, which she acknowledged as her departed brother's name. His reading went on for nearly an hour and I was amazed at how that time just flew. Dave was an amazing charismatic spirit and I felt very comfortable painting him back to life for his sister.

Nancy was able to understand everything that her brother spoke of and she validated everything for me as we chatted after I stopped the cd recorder. The only thing she couldn't understand was Dave having had a broken heart when he was in his early twenties. I just assumed that I missed somehow and I let it go when all of a sudden she blurted out, "Could it be that it was not a broken heart in a romantic way but an actual heart that was broken?" She said that Dave had found out when he was twenty two that he suffered from a heart defect that could not be repaired by surgery and that the doctors didn't know if he would live another day with it or another seventy years with it. She said this is why Dave chose to never get involved in any romantic relationships as he knew his days were numbered and he didn't want to put someone through that type of hurt. I thought to myself, what a beautiful unselfish young man he was. I apologized to her for missing what he was trying to get across through me, but in the end she understood exactly what he was trying to convey.

She went on to tell me that at the age of thirty nine Dave left his apartment on the Upper West Side of Manhattan and was just outside of Grand Central Terminal when he collapsed onto the sidewalk. He died instantly of a massive heart attack while on his way to meet an old friend coming in by train for dinner. One of the other things that Dave had said to his sister during her reading was that she needed to stop beating herself up for not saying goodbye to him. He told her, "We're family we never have to say goodbye." This one single statement from a brother in spirit to a sister still in the living had such a major impact on her that months later I ran into Nancy at another group reading event and she came over to thank me for her reading again. I told her, and I meant it when I said it, that it was my pleasure. I truly enjoyed meeting her brother and getting to converse with him as he was such a big hearted guy. He had been a living teddy bear.

Had I not trusted spirit that night to do the right thing for this brother and sister, I could have easily declined doing the reading as I was already at my supposed limit. This is why I always stress to student mediums: only you know how much energy you have to work with, never let anyone else tell you how much energy you have or don't have. They have no business doing that to you and they are most likely speaking from their own limitations. You and you alone with the help of your spirit workers will decide what your capabilities are in any given moment. Remember the quote earlier from Les Brown, "Never let someone else's opinion become your reality."

I was blessed to have worked with a teacher at Arthur Findlay College in England who was gracious enough to spend a few minutes with me personally and help me with my use of symbols and signs. I had been shown to use signs and symbols as a way of gathering the information from the spirit communicator and then paint the scenes into a picture for my sitter. This incredible medium at Stansted explained to me that sometimes it's just easier to simply ask the spirit for the information and make it more conversational than trying to decipher symbols. She changed my mediumship abilities that day. It took me a few weeks to adapt to the new techniques and even today I still do use some signs and symbols to gather information from my spirit communicators, but on the whole most of what I get from spirit at this point of my unfoldment is coming to me as imprints, visual imprints to my third eye, and sometimes an auditory name or comment. Spirit has taught me to not paint myself into any corners by limiting how they can get parts of the puzzle through to me for the loved ones I am reading for.

Any medium worth his weight in salt knows that you must constantly allow spirit to train you and at the same time knows that you are training spirit to work with you as well. It is an interactive process between the loved ones in spirit using what the medium has made available to them, to bring through evidence and messages for the loved ones still in the physical side of life.

It is incredibly important that the medium always remain in control of the actual reading. Those in spirit understand this and respect our process. Those on the spirit side are in control of what can be brought through the medium to the living recipient. This is what is meant by trusting in spirit, knowing that they are giving you real information that is necessary for the communication between the two worlds. There may be occasions where the sitter tries to control the reading and it will almost always be disastrous. The sitter does not have a link to the spirit world during the reading so there is no value in the medium allowing for the sitter to be in control. It can only hurt the quality of the reading and make the medium lose confidence in their gift and abilities. As my main teacher Janet Nohavec often says, "True mediumship is a perfect cocktail, all three ingredients are at work, the spirit communicator, the medium and the sitter." I have come to learn that all three components of a reading are important and any one of them can throw off a good reading. If the medium is too tired and not prepared, it can make for a less than stellar reading. If the link to the spirit world is not strong, then there will be little of value coming though. If the sitters or recipients do not truly want the best reading, they can actually limit what the medium can bring through.

Many of the old time twentieth century mediums said all too often that mediumship is a "grand experiment" each and every time. If a medium is giving the same messages over and over to different sitters it may be that the medium is tired or bored or has just gotten lazy and has not put in the effort with the continuing development of their mediumship. All working mediums are students for life. You must work on improving your relationship with spirit daily. Spirit wants us to become the best mediums we are capable of developing into. As a medium if you put in hard work and love, you will serve spirit honorably and help so many people. If you are lazy, you will be a medium who works without integrity. It's your choice, which type of medium would you like to be for serving spirit?

22 "I SEE DEAD PEOPLE" -THE SIXTH SENSE FILM

At least once during every conversation I have had with people I am asked if I see dead people in my mind's eye or with my eyes open. The straight answer is yes, to both.

I see spirit subjectively in almost every reading I do. I, like most other credible mediums, am mostly working clairsentiently during private one to one readings. I have found in my own experience that if I choose to work with my eyes closed I am able to receive more information clairvoyantly. There is also an increase in my clairaudient abilities as well when I close my eyes. That is the ability to hear directly from the spirit communicator in my mind's ear. Sometimes I will even hear spirit out loud. Even though I have been trained to work with my eyes open, looking directly at my sitter, I found this to be very limiting for my mediumship development. That is not to say that my way of working would be as effective for other developing mediums. It is up to each medium to find the styles and techniques that are most helpful to them in service to spirit work. For me, my mediumship expanded rapidly when I was no longer looking at my sitter. I feel that if you are looking at your sitter you consciously and subconsciously, are picking things up from your sitter. This is a form of cold reading and I have strived not to allow that method into my repertoire of how I serve spirit. I am aware of many mediums who work from a place of integrity that do work looking directly at their sitter. Every medium is in charge of what style of medium they become. I have experienced objective clairvoyance numerous times and have never been frightened by any of the "ghosts" I have seen with me eyes open. I do not believe in ghosts in the way that television and films have portrayed them. I also understand that there is an entire industry built on the premise that there are ghosts and that hauntings are happening at certain locations. I am not looking to enter into a debate as to whether ghosts exist or not, I'm not interested enough in this subject to make a career of it. I believe that we must come from a premise that there is intelligence on the other side, and I can find no intelligence in these hauntings.

I am aware that energy can never truly be destroyed and that all things will leave some trace evidence of their existence. This is what I feel is a viable explanation for "ghosts." I believe when we see a ghost, what we are actually seeing is due to either an increase in vibration or an increase in our sensitivity at that moment. This may explain why when someone sees a ghost it is only for a moment or two and not an extended period of time. I have also not heard of too many claims of people have an ongoing relationship with any particular ghost. When we do experience a ghost sighting it is usually a rarity, a fluke, something not of the norm, and we must accept that it happened and try not to turn it into something more than it actually was. People often personalize anything this rare and so it becomes more about them and their experience of it as opposed to the ghostly experience.

I have had less than a dozen ghost sightings that I feel were real and not from my imagination. One that stands out in my mind as being fairly incredible happened while I was attending a mediumship workshop in Kennebunkport Maine. It may have had something to do with the fact that there were about one hundred and twenty two mediums in a single space or that numerous passing of guests had occurred in that specific inn, as it was well over a hundred years old. Perhaps it was a combination of the two sets of circumstances.

I had spent thirty years as a working hairdresser and couldn't help but notice how beautiful the young woman with the most gorgeous natural blonde curls looked when she stood three rows ahead of me to ask the tutors a question. The room we were in for this class had a vaulted ceiling and was very spacious and comfortable. As this attractive woman asked her question my eyes were drawn up above her head and over a bit to the right of where she stood. In silhouette, like an old black and white photograph, I saw a gentleman walking across the room very slowly. I could see his face even though he was wearing a hat in the style of the nineteen-forties. He was pale and looked very safe and comfortable in this space. I never, even for a second, felt any fear or sense of alarm from his appearance. He slowly moved about twenty or so feet and moved his head slowly as if he was taking note of what was happening fifteen feet below his pathway. I turned my head and watched him fade away to my right. About thirty seconds later I saw three more figures, again slowly following the same pathway that he had just gone. It was two more men followed by a lady at the end of their procession. They were more visible to my eyes than she was. They also just faded as they moved to my right. The friend I was with at the course exclaimed to me, "You're seeing something, right?" I said, "Yes," and told her about it on the break which came up shortly thereafter.

A few days after that seminar ended someone from the group started a Facebook page that was limited to people who went through this class. Amazingly, as we all shared our experience of that long weekend there were dozens of stories similar to mine. None of us had seen what any of the others had seen but we all did have some sort of eyes-open clairvoyant experience. One woman shared that each morning she would rise before it was light out and head out for a morning walk of solitude which is her habit. She shared that there was a presence waiting for her, seated at the bottom of the staircase in the inn. As she walked pass this man in spirit she said to him, "Come on, let's go." For four days she said she had company on her strolls. Once back at the inn she would tell him to wait for her and she would see him tomorrow. She did say that he appeared in her room the first night and she nicely asked him not to come into her room as she would need to get a good night's sleep. He never came to her room again. It seems they are respectful and polite on the other side. I shared my experience with the group and all of us that had similar experiences all agreed that we never once felt anything other than a sense of friendship from these visitors. There was nothing threatening in the least about these visitations. This is what I mean when I speak about coming from a place of intelligence in the spirit world.

Had even one person freaked out and started screaming, I believe that there would have been no other visits from the spirit world in this manner of objective clairvoyance. I actually experienced a little bit of sadness when I left there after the weekend was over. I enjoyed communing with such great mediums from all over the country and a few from outside of the United States. I have to assume that spirit knew they would be welcomed in this very loving open group. I even felt bad for the folks that did not get to have that type of experience that weekend. I imagine spirit knew which mediums could handle it or would be the most available to them. I learned many different things that weekend, most of which was from the other mediums and not necessarily from the two teachers who were running the class. Interestingly, almost all of my sightings happened within a close space in time, all within a year.

I was sitting on the couch in a friend's house and she had lost an adult child to spirit a few months earlier. This was very early in my development as a medium and I looked towards her staircase and I saw her son climbing the stairs very slowly and with a sense of determination. What was odd about this visit was that he was not in context to the space of the room we were in. Although he appeared to be full in stature it was like he was about a hundred yards away yet the staircase was maybe ten feet from where I sat. He reminded me of a scaled down version of himself, maybe a quarter of his natural size when in the living. It was a most interesting and loving way to see him.

Later that same day I was standing inside of my tenant's apartment which is on the ground level of my home and I saw a man walking up the path and I did not recognize him. I was a little startled by his appearance and opened my tenant's door quickly to approach the man when he just faded away. I think because my demeanor was one of surprise and not all that welcoming that I may have scared off my visitor. I learned a valuable lesson that day and now I am always open and willing to have a visit from the other side. There need not be anything scary about sightings unless we add that part to the scenario from out active imaginations. Try to come from a place of common sense when dealing with and interacting with those in the spirit world. They are no longer physical, so there is never any need to worry about them hurting you. They are not physical and couldn't hurt you even if they wanted to, but they do not ever want to anyways.

I have heard the explanation that when we see a spirit with our eyes open that what we may actually be seeing is a stain of the energy left behind of that spirit's human physical body. It does sound plausible to me, but I don't know if there is ever any way to prove that theory in any scientific manner or test, but for some reason this idea does resonate with me.

I do believe that there are places where there may be a more concentrated pool of spirit energies. I have felt that energy while staying at Stansted Hall at The Arthur Findlay College in England. It is also been experienced by many guests staying at The Maplewood Hotel on the grounds of Lily Dale. Many people have heard what sounded like horses moving around on the floor above where they were trying to sleep. I have my own story of seeing a guest disappearing into a doorway which, when I got closer turned out to be a wall. She was not the least bit scary to me.

Over the years I have heard many stories from people about episodes that seemed very scary when it happened to them. I must admit I was somewhat skeptical of their accounts until it happened to me. I'm talking about the sensation of being held down by something and being unable to get up.

The first night that I spent in Stansted Hall in room 304, I was awakened from a deep sleep, jumping out of bed and seemingly boxing someone who was not there. I had some boxing training as a young man and know how to protect myself better than most people. I woke up my roommate by screaming, "Get off me, get off me!" I was throwing punches and woke up with my heart pounding and my adrenaline racing. It took me about an hour to calm down enough to fall back asleep. I literally felt like someone was laying full body weight on me and I couldn't wrestle them off of me.

I stayed at Stansted for two weeks that trip and was moved to the room directly next door for the second week as they had already booked my first room. About a year later when one of the tutors from The Arthur Findlay College was teaching a class at The Journey Within Church in New Jersey, she mentioned that there were two rooms at Stansted that seem to be haunted, room 304 and the room directly next to it. I can vouch for the authenticity of her statement.

Yet another tutor from the college was speaking about that phenomena and brought up an interesting perspective that I had never thought of. His take on the sensation of someone lying on you and holding you down, that feeling of temporary paralysis and not being able to free oneself, was that maybe it was one of your spirit guides trying to protect you. They would hold you back for a short period of time so that you may miss something harmful in the not too distant future. Again, it seems plausible but that was the only time I had ever reacted in such a strong negative manner to something unseen. For me, the jury is still out on this one.

There was another student who shared her experience of being in a single room in a hallway where there were no other sleeping rooms but just a staircase and a bathroom. She said it was a noisy room because of the people using the bathroom, but even more because of the strange voices she heard coming out of the corners of her room. I asked her if it could've been people in the hallway or in the bathroom, but she said no it was a constant conversation. She inquired at the front desk, but there were no other rooms for her to switch to. She bought earplugs and made the best of it for the week she was there. She has never returned to Stansted Hall. I would gladly go anytime, but I would be careful about which room I stayed in.

23 STAYING ALIVE

All mediums are psychics but rarely are psychics mediums. Although many psychics claim to have mediumistic abilities, I have never actually seen one. The subtle quality of the energies a medium works with takes many years and many readings to come to understand the nuances of your own individual energies. There are times that a medium believes they are working with spirit but in actuality they are working from their own psychic abilities, especially when they are still in the early stages of their mediumistic development. The two differing types of energy go hand in hand with each other and can sometimes be mistaken for each other.

I was doing a reading with a wonderful sitter at her office in New Jersey once, and I didn't feel a shift in my energy when I gave her a very specific name, Ernie Douglas and said that I believed she would know him from town. I was hearing, "Ernie Douglas town." Even though her reading had been stellar up to that point, she had no idea of any one named Ernie Douglas, certainly not from the town she lived in or for that matter from the town her office was in either. I asked her to remember the name and place and finished her reading. About a week later, I received a call from this sitter telling me that she was on a business trip and her rental car broke down. The person that the rental company had sent to help her handed her his invoice to bring back to the rental company after he got her car running again. It was a simple dead battery and she was not even late to her meeting that morning. He was quite taken aback when she laughed aloud when she looked at his invoice. The mechanical service person's name was Ernie Douglaston. She said she couldn't wait to tell me. I had given her something from her future, not from her past or spirit loved ones in that case. When she tried to explain to him why she had laughed he simply rolled his eyes, "He probably thought I was some flaky chick from back east."

Mediums and healers are usually very aware of the energies that are around them. Most people are aware of energy and aren't even aware of that fact. If you come into a room where the people already in there have just had a fight or an argument you can usually feel that something just isn't right or comfortable in that room. That is you feeling the energies of that room or those people. That is what a medium does, but on a much higher more attuned level. There are times I come into a space where I am to do multiple readings and there may be as many as ten people in that room, yet sometimes one person in particular will catch my attention and it is usually because I sense something "off" with their energy. Many times I will ask the host about that person, and there have even been times that I will take that person as my last sitting of the event so that they cannot throw off my energy which might give the other sitters a reading less than what I would want for them.

Have you ever met someone and for no reason that you can quickly identify, you just don't like that person or you are suspicious of them for no apparent reason. That is you trusting your "gut" feelings. That is just another version of you being perceptive to the energies of others. Many law enforcement personnel rely on their abilities of intuition to help them in their work while investigating crimes. Ironically, it has been pointed out to me that when I trust what I call my "gut" feeling I am usually wrong, but when I classify my feeling as a "sense" of something, I am rarely wrong. As a medium, I rely and trust my "sense" of things far more often that most people.

Have you ever noticed that some people you have in your life are what I refer to as energy vampires? These people can be just so needy that they suck the life out of you the way a vampire sucks the blood out of its victims. It is nice to be helpful to people, however, you must set boundaries with these energy vampires as they can literally make you sick from the amount of your energy they can absorb. You will never be able to satisfy their needs for more. I feel sorry for those who are involved in ongoing relationships with this type of a person. You need to limit the time you give to these types of people as they will constantly come to draw from the well of your good intentions. All wells run dry eventually unless you find ways to replenish your own energy. This is where just being in nature can be so helpful. Meditation to keep yourself grounded will also make a world of difference if you happen to be involved in a relationship with an energy vampire. Try to remember that no one can take anything from you without you letting them do it. No one has any powers that can enable them to take your energy unless you allow them to do so. That is what I meant by saying that you must set boundaries because these types of people struggle with boundary issues.

One of the many blessings in my life has been where I have my home. I have lived in the same house for twenty five years and it has proven to be a wonderful place to develop my mediumship. I live on a quiet tree-lined street with wooded areas in front of and behind my house. My house abuts the property of a former Catholic College that has been here for well over a century. There are three houses that surround my house in a triangle. All three of these houses have housed Catholic nuns for more than fifty years. I believe I live in a very energetic place due to the number of prayers that have been said here for well over a century. I think there is residual energy concentrated in places of worship. That is why people usually feel a sense of calm when they sit in a large older cathedral like St. Patrick's in New York City. I have always been drawn to places of worship to sit and meditate.

This is why a place like Lily Dale New York has become so magical in its energy. Most people who visit Lily Dale notice a change in the feel of the energy when you arrive and how it feels different when you leave. I have heard people speak of there being a vortex of energy at Lily Dale and other places in New York State such as the Hudson Valley Region. I'm not proficient in my knowledge of how or what makes a vortex, but I can tell you that I do feel differing energies when I go to certain places. My home is one of these on a much smaller scale.

This may be one of the reasons that my mediumship keeps progressing at a rate that others have remarked on being a little quicker than most. I don't know if it necessarily has, but I do know that your own development is directly linked to your own spiritual growth, and that it takes long hours and hard work to accomplish that. We live in a society at a time in history where we want everything in sound bites and even our language has been shortened to accommodate how we communicate on our mobile phones and computer devices. There is no shortcut to mediumship development. If you are serious about spending your life in service to those in the spirit world, you must be willing and available to put in the hard work and devotion that it demands. The rewards of being able to help so many others who are suffering and struggling in their lives are well worth the sacrifices you are called on to make. My only regret is that I didn't recognize my abilities much earlier in life as I could have been helpful so much longer. They say that when the student is ready the teacher appears. I am so happy I chose not to play hooky any longer in my own life.

I have become friendly with my neighbors who happen to be nuns. They are lovely women who chose to live a life that most of us would never even consider. I have great respect for their devotion to their work and their belief systems. They often tell me that they are praying for me and it always makes me smile for I am so open to accepting their prayers and using those prayers to help power my mediumship in serving the needs of others. I have been so fortunate to have gotten to know so many wonderful mediums over the years. If one contacts me and asks me to send them energy because they have a difficult reading coming up I will always send energy to them. Just as at times I have sent texts to my friends asking them for a little extra energy as I have a group that night that may be a little difficult. I know that I can count on them sharing their energy with me as well. This is how we serve spirit, for the highest good of all involved. Mediums in general, if they are not coming from a place of ego, can be some of the most beautiful souls walking this Earth. I am proud to have the opportunity to have worked with, and developed with, some amazing human beings who give without a selfish bone in their bodies. These are the everyday angels!

If there is one thing I have learned it is that all mediums, and especially student mediums, need to practice constantly to really stretch their gifts. After you have gone through your close friends and relatives who are you going to practice with? What I did was to create a series of phone readings as practice. I asked friends to pass my name and number to someone they knew but that I knew nothing about or even better had never met or even heard of before. That person was to call me and I would do a free phone reading with them. The only thing that I did ask from the sitter on the other end of the phone was a promise that they would then pass my name and number onto someone else and so on. I was able to have a never ending phone chain of sitters to practice with. I would sometimes do five or six of these practice readings a week.

I have heard people question whether a phone reading was just as good as an in person one on one reading. I have found in my experience that there is no difference in the quality of the readings done on the phone from those done face to face. An example I can share with you is from a phone practice reading I did with a woman from New York City by the name of Mary Jane.

I had never heard anything about Mary Jane as she was a friend of a friend of a friend. You cannot get much further distance than that. Mary Jane called me and I asked her not to tell me anything but to give me a phone number and a time that would work for her to be able to sit and have a reading with me over the phone. I called her the next day at the time we had worked out and her reading was wonderful. This was a reading very early on in my development and I believe that Spirit gives you certain readings at certain times to help your mediumship to develop and to grow.

After saying hello to Mary Jane I immediately felt the presence of a spirit who felt like an older man who had white hair and he felt like he was her dad. The spirit communicator showed me a hand pulling on a belt and that meant to me that he had lost a lot of weight and that he had cancer at the time of his passing from physical to spirit. I said to her that her dad was showing me the month of August as being significant. I then felt there was a younger Italian man with this older man. The younger man was showing me that he was obsessed with losing the hair on the top of his head. I then heard the expression an Americanized version of an Italian name. The last thing I saw before I asked for validation from Mary Jane was The John Travolta character from Saturday Night Fever walking down the street in Brooklyn in his white disco suit carrying a can of paint and heading into the paint store in the movie, all the while I was hearing the song "Staying Alive" by The Bee Gees.

Mary Jane acknowledged that her dad was indeed in spirit and he had a head of shocking white hair, she also said that he did lose a great amount of weight due to the cancer condition he was struggling with before it took him to spirit. She said his name was August but everyone called him Augie, there was my August connection. When I mentioned about the younger guy obsessed with losing his hair she laughed and said that's my brother-in-law Pete, but we called him Guido. There was the Americanized Italian name. When I mentioned the scene of John Travolta going into the paint store in Brooklyn in the film Saturday night Fever, Mary Jane started to scream, "Shut the **** up" over and over.

After a few minutes of her screaming and cursing I could hear people coming to her aid over the phone. Mary Jane got back on the phone and said to me, "Oh my God you have my father with you." I replied, "Yes I do." She then went on to tell me that her dad, along with his brothers, owned the paint store in Brooklyn that was used in the film Saturday Night Fever. She had met John Travolta in her father's store when he was there filming the movie. She was so amazed and blown away by the information that I had shared that she needed to get off the phone as she was in her office at work saying she would call me back soon to finish the reading. I never heard back from Mary Jane. I guess she got what she needed and for her there was no longer a need for any other contact.

I have had similar readings on the phone with great evidence like that, so I would have to conclude that there is no difference in a phone reading as opposed to an in person reading. I have heard similar observations from other credible mediums that I respect. Mental mediumship is a mind to mind communication therefore I can understand logically that you would not have to be in the same space when the reading is happening. I always record my in person readings and I also record all of my phone readings. I mail the sitter the cd after the reading is over. I find that recording any reading you participate in as a medium is essential in that it is a reminder that you are responsible for every word that comes out of your mouth in a reading. The recording is a record of that person's individual reading. This type of discipline forces you to become more accountable in your mediumship which in turn raises the quality of your readings. It is truly a win-win situation for all involved. To become a credible medium you must strive to work from a place of integrity in your mediumship, recording your readings helps this along and I recommend that you embrace this process.

I recently gave a lecture in front of a group of college students and faculty. The energy of some of the individuals in the room was quite distinctive and somewhat hard to understand. I learned after the lecture and demonstration that many of the people attending that day were extremely impoverished financially. The idea behind my appearing before this group was quite interesting to me. The faculty was operating a program that exposed these wonderful but poor people to things they wouldn't normally be exposed to, such as a psychic medium who speaks on all things Spiritual. I was quite moved by their interest in my story of how I became who I am and the work that I do. In the end, it was I who was truly the student and not the teacher as I learned an important lesson that day.

All people are interested in their own spiritual growth. They all have questions about where they fit in this world. It didn't matter that there were little or limited means, what mattered to members of this audience was that they had a hunger for knowledge about things beyond their individual situations. I was impressed by their desire to learn about spirituality. This was quite the lesson for me, as up till this point I had an unconscious thought process that people who were struggling like many of these attendees didn't have time to think about the bigger picture. I believed they were so caught up in survival mode that they were not available to yearnings beyond paying today's bills and keeping a roof over their head. I guess I had been projecting my own version of survival onto them, yet here we were, talking about afterlife communications and where do we go after we leave this life.

I was scheduled to lecture for an hour. I left two and a half hours after I started. I was eager to share with them and they were like young sponges drinking up my stories and experiences. For the last forty minutes of my time with this group I moved into demonstrating mediumship for them.

I felt an older man in spirit who was very happy to have the opportunity to connect back to his loved one in the room. I shared that he had passed after an illness that affected his ability to breathe and especially at the very end of his life. I looked at this very sweet lady and asked her if this gentleman belonged to her, already knowing that he did. She coyly smiled and nodded her head yes. She was shy and this could make it difficult to maintain this connection but I pressed on as this man was here and he had a sense of determination that came through quite strongly. I gave her the name of Jackson but told her that I believed it was the name of a street and not a person, I also said that I believed there were other Presidential named streets nearby and that Jefferson could be the next street over. She became exuberant and said yes her grandfather lived on Jackson Street when she was a little girl and that Jefferson was the next street over from there. He then told me that there was something funny about her driving test. I asked if this was correct and she said that something funny did happen when her grandfather took her to take her driving examination.

The group was now very engaged and I felt his connection getting even stronger. This is what we mediums call the spirit is moving closer to me. I said to her, "I'm not sure why but he is giving me two names, the name Ray, and I feel like it is Ray Charles, and the other name is a nickname I believe, but spelled Hunny." With this piece of information she became excited and blurted out that her legal name was indeed Hunny, spelled exactly that way and that she listens to Ray Charles all of the time. The only way I could make sense of the Ray Charles connection was that her grandfather may come around her when she listens to his music. She was so happy to have heard from him and the others in the room applauded which kind of made me embarrassed but in a nice way.

Bringing that message through in front of that group had a profound impact on some of the people attending that day. I have since heard from numerous people and some have booked appointments in the hope of having their own connection to loved ones in spirit or as they called it, their aha moment.

I have been asked to come back to that college to give another lecture and demonstration of mediumship. I took that as a nice compliment to be asked back, but more importantly, I had learned a valuable lesson and they had engaged in an opportunity that expanded their awareness. Spirit sure does work in some interesting ways.

The more often I work with Spirit and the energy that is used in mental mediumship, I find, in my limited experience, that I am just happier in general. It is a nice by-product of doing the work for something you love so deeply and knowing that on various levels you are having a positive impact in people's lives. I am truly blessed to have found my life's purpose, to live a life in service to spirit and to all human beings in the physical world. I can think of no greater accomplishment that can bring me this much joy and satisfaction. As I am in my late fifties I have paused to think, too bad I didn't live this kind of life sooner, but the truth is, I am living it at the right time, now. I would not have been worldly or mature enough to handle the awesome responsibility of service to the spirit world before this point in my life. My seriousness of purpose would not have been at this level until I arrived at this place at this time to bring the wisdom and discipline needed to do this work, and I love it!!!

Forgiveness, love, and compassion are recurring words you will find in my writings as they are the building blocks for the foundation of humanity. Each person is equipped with these most beautiful gifts to share with other human beings. The sad irony for many in this physical life is that they never truly learn the real value of these gifts until some tragedy has occurred and that tragedy is usually the loss of someone we love.

I am asked quite often to help a sitter navigate their future. As I have heard it said from another medium, I cannot tell your future but I can tell you what is going to happen. There are rarely any predictions of future events that are one hundred percent accurate. Some of the more famous psychics generally make yearly predictions and then slap themselves on the back over and over upon some of their predictions coming true. What they fail to share with you is the ninety percent of the predictions they made that did not come true. It is a form of blanketing the masses and then only pointing up the successes and disregarding the missed predictions. We have been given the beautiful blessing of having free will so every single moment and interaction we are a part of can change and constantly does, and that is why you should use your own common sense and know that nothing stays the same forever. Change is always happening, so how can anyone truly accurately predict your future? Even the great Nostradamus has worded things in such a way that his accuracy is determined by how much you would like him to be correct.

I and most mediums who take to the pen to tell their stories are culpable of this as well. I have shared with you many experiences and I will admit that my memory is far better telling the stories of my remarkable readings as opposed to sharing the readings that were not quite as memorable. I am human and I do have an ego, so I apologize if I appear to portray myself as the most incredible medium walking this planet. I am not. There is always someone who will be the better reader for a particular sitter at a particular moment. I stand behind all that I have shared in these writings as being factually correct and drawn from my own memories with an aim for accuracy. I have changed names and even the gender on a few of the stories I have shared here with you so that the privacy of the individuals who truly own these stories may best be protected. I have done my best to be an engaging storyteller and to, hopefully, open your eyes and your hearts to the possibilities of that which I experience on a daily basis with the spirit side of life. All beings continue on after what we know of as physical death. We are energy and energy can never be destroyed, it will always live on. We are spirits first having a human experience in a very difficult place and time. We are constantly growing and learning in an evolving process that we have the ultimate control of. We are responsible for ourselves and our actions. We are also responsible as a whole, along with all other human beings, to everyone else as there is no separation between people that are spirits first.

If we learn to value the things that are deeply important in our lives here we will grow on a much grander level in our life beyond the physical. All of life is in constant motion so we should learn to embrace the changes that happen around us and with us. Even in our more difficult moments, we are never alone. There are people here in the physical world and always loved ones on the spirit side of life who are ready to show us love and support no matter what we are experiencing. Being alone is an illusion humans have deceived themselves with. It is not possible to be truly alone as we are a part of a much larger group. There are spirits that are connected to us in ways that we may not be able to comprehend with the limitations of our thinking brains at this time in evolution, but we should come to a place of trust that they will always be there for us if we choose to be connected with them.

Many of the lessons that are present in this time of history have to do with love and tolerance of all people. When we come to appreciate and embrace our differences as strongly as we currently choose to do just the opposite, we will have evolved to a place that will be closer to our truest spiritual nature. That which is at the core of every single human being who has ever been alive or will ever be alive will become the spiritual path of life that has always been available to us and we will be closer to our God of choice. Our spark of divinity that is the driving force of all human nature will take us closer to that which we call the light. For it is in this light that we are all one and as we have always been connected, we will fulfill our purpose. This is the meaning of life that we so long for every single day of our human experience and more importantly, our spiritual life.

All love is valued and important to us. For us to become part of The One we must surrender to the idea that we are and always have been spirits based in love. This is why we strive our entire lifetime searching and trying to hold onto one form or another of love. Our loved ones in spirit now exist in a place of pure unconditional love and we will all be there again one day. You are a beautiful sunflower raising your face of love to shine in the light that sustains and grows us. Feel the love deep down in your roots and know you are loved and that you are love.

Open your eyes and your heart and look to the heavens, for this is where you shall be known by your light.

A DECEMBER MOON

The next page shares the poem I was working on the day that I had my first spirit communication. I believe that I wrote the beginning and the ending of this poem. The middle section that are in italics may have been inspired writing or possibly spirit writing. I have no recollection of writing those words in italics.

A December Moon

Will always remind me of
his face.
Full and natural,
Deep in contemplation,
sometimes sad.
Only photos now exist,
The photos will age, he,
forever young.
Many times alone,
Even in a room filled with
people.
Full on internal chatter,
Somewhat ambiguous, and
hovering.
All that drew near,
Taken in by his brilliance.
At arm's length,
Seemed to be his comfort space.
Those that he loved the most,
Often brought closer,
And also kept at a further
distance.
A paradox existence.

We could not understand,
The world in which he thought.
Some things so simple to him,
But complicated beyond our grasp.
Some things so easy for us,
Difficult for his brilliant mind.
A paradox existence.
A December moon rises
higher,
The air is crisp and clean from
the cold.
Now there is quiet,
Quiet is for the thinkers.
A December moon,
Will always remind me of his
face,
Full and natural,
Deep in thoughts, no longer
sad.

SUGGESTED BOOKS

- Anderson, George. *Lessons From The Light: Extraordinary Messages of Comfort and Hope from the Other Side.*
  New York : Putnam, 1999.

- Anderson, George. *Walking In The Garden of Souls: George Anderson's Advice From the Hereafter, For Living in the Here and Now.*
  New York : G.P. Putnam's Sons, 2001.

- Anderson, George and Joel Martin and Patricia Romanowski Bashe. *We Don't Die: George Anderson's Conversations With the Other Side.*
  New York : G.P. Putnam's Sons, 1988.

- Borg, Marcus J. and Mark Powelson and Ray Riegert. *The Lost Gospel Q: The Original Sayings of Jesus.*
  Berkeley, Calif. : Ulysses Press, 1996.

- Dykshoorn, M.B. and Russell H Felton. *My Passport Says Clairvoyant.*
  New York : Hawthorn Books, 1974.

- Ford, Will with Linda Muir. *The Seeing Eye, The Feeling Heart*
  London : produced on behalf of the Spiritualists' National Union by Tudor Press, 1993.

- Giesemann, Suzanne. *The Priest and the Medium : The Amazing True Story of Psychic Medium B. Anne Gehman and Her Husband, Former Jesuit Priest Wayne Knoll*
  Carlsbad, Calif. : Hay House, 2009.

- Kubler-Ross, Elisabeth. *On Death and Dying.* New York : Macmillan, 1969.

- Nohavec, Janet and Suzanne Giesemann. *Where Two Worlds Meet: How to Develop Evidential Mediumship* San Diego, CA : Aventine Press, 2010.

- Owen, Lionel. *Please God Why?: Ego and Spirit – The Conflict* HP Comunicacao Editora , 2008.

- Silver Birch Books by various authors

- Smith, Gordon. *Through My Eyes.* London : Hay House, 2006.

- Smith, Gordon. *The Unbelievable Truth: A Medium's Insider Guide to the Unseen World* London : Hay House, 2004.

- Stemman, Roy. *Spirit Communication: A Comprehensive Guide to the Extraordinary World of Mediums, Psychics and the Afterlife.* London : Piatkus, 2005.

- Weisberg, Barbara.*Talking To The Dead: Kate and Maggie Fox and the Rise of Spiritualism.* San Francisco : Harper, 2004.

CONTACT

compassionatemedium.com

jake@compassionatemedium.com

facebook.com/compassionatemedium

914-227-5398.

.

JAKE SAMOYEDNY

Jake Samoyedny is The Compassionate Medium. Born a medium, he has trained with some of the best mediums alive today. Jake has also studied at the prestigious Arthur Findlay College for Psychical Studies in Stansted, England. He is a member of The Spiritualist National Union International and a member of The Lily Dale Assembly. Jake is a Registered Medium at Lily Dale, America's oldest Spiritualist Community. He is a member and a demonstrating medium at The Journey Within Church. Jake lives a spiritual life and has devoted himself to serving Spirit through Evidential Mediumship, bringing comfort to those searching for proof that our lives and bonds of love are everlasting.

Jake resides with his two children and does readings in the suburbs north of New York City and can also be found living and serving Spirit in Lily Dale, New York during the summer months. To learn more about Jake Samoyedny "The Compassionate Medium" please visit his website at: compassionatemedium.com

Made in the USA
Lexington, KY
29 May 2014